Betty Miller
9060 Alleghany Rd
Corfu, NY 14036-9765

HALF HEAVEN
HALF HEARTACHE

AN INCREDIBLE JOURNEY

By: Robert E. Alexander

xulon
PRESS

Copyright © 2008 by Robert E. Alexander

Half Heaven Half Heartache
An Incredible Journey
by Robert E. Alexander

Printed in the United States of America

ISBN 978-1-60791-094-7

All rights reserved solely by the author. The author guarantees all contents are original and do not infringe upon the legal rights of any other person or work. No part of this book may be reproduced in any form without the permission of the author. The views expressed in this book are not necessarily those of the publisher.

Unless otherwise indicated, Bible quotations are taken from The King James Version of the Bible.

www.xulonpress.com

Paul & Betty Lou,

May GOD bless you
my dear brother and
sister in Jesus.

Judge Alexander
Job 19:25
John 3:16
I Peter 2:9

WHAT THEY ARE SAYING

—⟋⟍—

When I look at the impact one man's life can have, especially a man that has gone through incredible life experiences, I look at the life of Judge Robert Alexander. Here is a man of great humility, courage and obedience in bringing not only the Truth of Jesus Christ to his readers but the grace that abounds in the Lord. I know Judge Alexander up close and personal. His life, this book, and his impact are the real deal. Read it and pass it on to someone you care about. You will be blessed!

Dr. Gary Rosberg
America's Family Coaches,
Co-Author (with wife, Barbara), 6 Secrets to a Lasting Love
Radio Show Co-Host, Co-founder with Barbara of: The
*   Great Marriage Experience*

It has been my great pleasure to personally know and observe the fabulous way our Lord has used the life and testimony of Judge Robert Alexander. He is my friend but more importantly he is a great friend and servant of Jesus and of lost souls everywhere. God has used him greatly and the half has yet been told. He is the real McCoy with an enormous passion for broken lives which he knows first hand can only be restored by the wonderful grace of God. You will be touched and encouraged as you read this miraculous story of how God is and has used this servant of our Lord.

Dr. Fletcher A. Brothers
Founder and Director Freedom Village USA

The greatest miracle is when God changes a life. The transformation of Robert Alexander is a miracle of God's grace and His power. It tells the world that there is no such thing as a hopeless cause. Someone once said, "You can't unscramble scrambled eggs!" Well after you read "Half Heaven, Half Heartache" you will realize that Jesus Christ through the power of His Holy Spirit can unscramble, scrambled eggs, because that is exactly what He did in the life of Robert Alexander. Now available in written form this book will lift your faith to a place where you can truly say "All things are possible to Him who believes." As a personal friend of Brother Alexander I can testify to the fact that Jesus Christ is living within him and he truly has been redeemed by the Blood of Jesus!

Michael Chorey,
Pastor of CrossRiver Church
Director of Joshua Revolution Youth Ministry

As an attorney whose practice is limited to the defense of those accused of crimes, I have appeared in countless Courts throughout New York State. Judge Robert Alexander is one the most able and competent jurists that I have had the pleasure of appearing before. He is always prepared and fully versed regarding the case before him. He treats every defendant with dignity and respect. He adheres to and respects the individual's rights, especially the presumption of innocence. Most significantly he treats everyone as individuals whose backgrounds and life stories are important. Judge Alexander metes out justice with a firm yet compassionate hand. He imposes a jail sentence when called for but he does so in a manner that would have been approved by Abraham Lincoln who said, "I have always found that mercy bears richer fruits than strict justice."

Michael Mohun,
Attorney at Law

When you read anything about Robert Alexander, you will find courage, humility and an overwhelming sincerity to help humanity. His core values emanate from everything he does and relate to whatever he involves himself in. What is even more amazing is that this humility stands within the shadows of the Christ who saved him, and that he is well aware of.

Pastor Martin K. Macdonald
The City Church
Batavia, New York

CONTENTS

—ᴍ—

Prologue xix

Tomorrow's Promise 23

Friends, Family, and Folly 29

Culture Shock..37

A Second Chance 49

The Plot Thins Out...57

Becoming So Many People..............................69

Here Comes The Night 77

The Wild Blue Yonder.....................................89

The Wild Wild West..99

Work Hard, Play Harder................................111

The Shadows Darken.....................................123

Bikers, Babes, and Bloodshed 135

The Long Road Home........................145

Playing to Win........................159

Broken is as Broken Does........................169

Falling Forward........................179

The Razor's Edge........................187

After All These Years........................201

The Gates of Hell Shall Not Prevail 209

God's Mighty Hand........................219

Both Sides of the Bars........................231

Here Comes Judge "A"........................241

Amen........................251

Afterward: Are You the One?........................261

DEDICATION

—⚬⚬—

The following story, *Half Heaven Half Heartache*, is my story, the autobiography of the Reverend and Judge Robert E. Alexander. It is a testimony to the saving grace and forgiveness offered by the sacrificial atonement through the blood of Jesus Christ, and is dedicated to those tormented souls who, like me, that blood has rescued. It also stands in recognition of those very special people who prayed me out of darkness into HIS marvelous light.

I want to leave this manuscript as a legacy so my descendants will know who and what I was; a desperate man who found peace.

In the love of Christ Jesus,

Robert E. Alexander
Corfu, New York
September, 2008

> *Come unto me, all ye that labor and are heavy laden, and I will give you rest. Take my yoke upon you, and learn of me; for I am meek and lowly in heart: and ye shall find rest unto your souls.*
>
> *Matthew 11:28-29.*

ACKNOWLEDGEMENTS

—ᵐ—

*H*alf Heaven Half Heartache could not have been written without the love and support of my wife, Gerry Ellen. For 36 years she has patiently stood by my side as a dedicated helpmate. Her faith in God has been a constant source of inspiration as we have served the Lord Jesus Christ together these 22 years.

I am continually challenged by the selfless manner in which she pours her life out to God and others. God knew we would need each other to conquer our wrecked lives. Thank you Jesus. I love you Gerry Ellen.

To Bob, Jenny, Brandon, Brian, Brandi, and Joshua. Words can not come close to expressing how much I love you. I pray that I have become a Christian Dad you can be proud of.

So many others have given sacrificially of their time, talents, and energy to help this dream come true. The professionalism, editorial efforts, and encouragement of Rick Kern have been invaluable. Thank you for your tireless dedication in making my life story into the book I prayed it would be.

Gloria Chapman's editorial help and lasting friendship have been a constant source of inspiration, as have Dan Nichols' advice and support.

The friendship and love of Paul and Toni Cook have enriched my life immeasurably, and words woefully fail to express my appreciation to Gary and Barb Rosberg for being such wonderful examples of Christian love and humility. I also want to thank Don and Jan, and Cutie Pie Seaver for there help and friendship.

To Matt and Patty Gambino, thank you for your love and testimony to God's grace.

Robby, Gail, Katelyn, Heath, and the Living Proof Band, your sacrifice and godly example continue to inspire and bless me.

Above all, thank you Jesus for saving my wretched soul.

FORWARD

—〰—

I first met Judge Robert Alexander via a phone message, followed by a video tape in the mail, and then personally a number of years later. Let me explain.

During the Father's Day weekend of 1997, I had the privilege of speaking at Promise Keepers in Buffalo, New York. Rich Stadium was teaming with over 27,000 men. The year before, at the RCA Dome in Indianapolis, I brought my wife, Barb, up on the stage and washed her feet in front of over 65,000 men. I didn't wash her feet because I thought it would make a good word picture. I washed her feet because Jesus writes in John 13:17 *Now that you know these things you will be blessed if you do them.* Likely, as every man and woman reading Robert Alexander's book desires to be blessed, so did I. So I was faithful to do what Jesus told me to do. I also promised God that if I ever spoke at a Promise Keepers again... I would take care of some unfinished business and wash my two daughter's feet as well. A year later, in Buffalo, God fulfilled that opportunity and I made good on my promise. That is where Judge Alexander and I first connected.

He was one of the men in the stadium. As God often does, when one man is attempting to be found faithful, it can become contagious. Bob Alexander had caught the bug and wanted to be blessed. He returned home-with a mission in his heart-to take care of some unfinished business with his own family, on Father's Day, 1997. Following dinner in his home, he gathered the mother who adopted him, his wife, two of his daughters, one of his sons, and a grandchild and blessed them by speaking a blessing over them and then washing their feet. He also had the wherewithal to put a video camera on his son in law's shoulder who caught the whole thing on video. The Judge sent it to me, I watched it in my home, and hence have shown it to tens of thousands of other men and women who want to be blessed by honoring Jesus and washing the feet of their families. The story of Judge Alexander's faithfulness has impacted thousands and moved many men and women to take care of unfinished business in their own lives.

This may be a strange forward to a book but it gives the backdrop of the man whose book you hold in your hands. I have met Judge Alexander. I have served alongside of him in ministering to men in his community. I have stood in his hospital room with some of his children during a stressful time. I have watched him in person minister to hundreds in my hometown as my guest, and his hometown when I was his guest. I have seen the tears flow countless times down countless sets of cheeks of broken and contrite hearts wanting to do the right thing and bless their families by following his lead in humbling themselves to wash the feet of their families.

In this book you read the word of Judge Robert Alexander as if he were standing in the room with you speaking them. This once hard hearted, hard headed, me-oriented man, has humbled himself, and surrendered to Jesus as Lord and Savior. Today he's a hero in the faith. He is a man's man. He is a tender man. He is a Godly man. He is a husband, father, and grandfather that is sold out to the Lord and speaking into the hearts of all who will listen about the hope we have in Jesus: including you and me.

As you read this book you will see the drama unfold: from days of drunken rages, to ministering to Mark David Chapman and David Berkowitz in prison. You will read of a reconciliation with his birth mother, the faithful prayers of his beloved wife that were answered when Bob accepted Jesus, and learn of the legacy that he is leaving behind that will glorify Christ long after he is in heaven. I am one of Judge Robert Alexander's greatest fans. And I sense when you read this testimony you will be too.

Guard Your Heart,
Dr. Gary and Barb Rosberg
America's Family Coaches
Authors, Radio Program Co-Hosts, and grateful grand-
    parents of five!

PROLOGUE

—‿∭‿—

It was June, 1945 and World War II had raged for four long years. The war's forbidding toll left no home unscathed and sacrifice had been the American way. As young men went to war women replaced them in the industrial factories that were grinding out the critically needed military equipment. Rosie the riveter became the poster girl for the effort.

One of those riveters Gertrude Faulring, was fighting another battle. And as she made her way to the lady's lounge in the Curtis Wright Airplane Modification Factory, her heart ached. She was medically unable to bear children and had been praying for a baby to adopt for a long time. Her emotions spilled over into tears as she noticed a pregnant woman sitting near the corner of the room slumped over crying in despair. Compassion flooded her heart as she approached the woman and asked, "Why are you crying?"

Slowly looking up, the woman explained that her husband had died and she was now married to a man who was an alcoholic and a wretch of a person. She sobbed as she shared that her 15 year old daughter Marge was also pregnant. And when the young man who fathered Marge's child learned that she was pregnant, he hastily returned to his home in Pennsylvania where another girl, also pregnant with his child, awaited.

"What am I going to do? Marge is due to have her baby in early October." The woman anguished at the thought of bringing her baby into a home with an alcoholic husband, much less Marge's baby.

Gert could barely get the words out, "I can't have children. Would you consider letting my husband, John, and I adopt Marge's baby?" She explained that, they were "Born Again Christians" and had been praying for a child to adopt. Gert also shared that her extended family were also Christians including her father, mother, brother, and sister-in-law.

From that fateful June, 1945 encounter it was arranged for Marge to live with Gert's brother and sister-in-law, Edwin and Adeline Theon, until the baby was born. The adoption document contained two provisions: First, John and Gertrude Faulring would become the child's parents with the birth certificate declaring them the *biological* mother and father. Second, Marge and her family would be permanently prohibited from contacting the Faulring's or the child.

When Marge went to live with Ed and Adeline Theon, she quickly realized that they were wonderful Christian people. They treated Marge very tenderly never saying one disparaging word about her being 15 years old and pregnant. In 1945 it was a terrible social blemish on a family and shameful for a young girl to become pregnant out of wedlock. Adeline was a kind woman who flooded Marge with tender loving care. Her wonderful Christian spirit became such a testimony that Marge was led to know Adeline's Jesus Christ as her own personal Savior.

However, when Marge went into labor she experienced a rude awaking. The nurses at the hospital treated her with contempt, ignoring her painful cries and responded with terse and cruel remarks, "Shame on you," they said condescendingly, "you know what you did and now you're suffering the consequences!" Marge felt totally abandoned as she lay in that delivery room. Indescribable fear and anguish filled her heart as she thought of her baby being taken from her and given to strangers. Questions raced through her mind, would they love, protect, and care for my baby like I would?

Her grief became almost unbearable upon hearing the first helpless cries of the baby boy she delivered, only to have him whisked away while the nurses blocked her strained attempts to see him. Marge longed to hold him, and at least say I love you and goodbye. However, within moments his cries faded and he was gone. And there, in the throes of her heartbreak, she vowed that someday before she died, she would reach out and lovingly hold the child she couldn't hold today.

The only thing Marge was told, as she was given a bouquet of roses sent from the Faulrings, was that his name was going to be Bobby. Because she lived with the Theons while she was pregnant, no one in her family except her mother knew she had a baby that was adopted out, not even her older sister. Marge's mother firmly demanded that she never say one word about having had a baby.

It was agonizing for Marge when she returned home and there was her baby brother, Jack, being loved and nurtured by her mother and older sister. Her heart wrenched in pain as she held Jack but could only imagine what her Bobby looked like and if someone was lovingly holding him. She wondered if her heartache would ever end.

CHAPTER 1

TOMORROW'S PROMISE

—⁓—

For me, Robert Edwin Faulring (Bobby) life was wonderful. Daddy John and Momma Gert moved into the family homestead in Alden, New York, where we lived with Grandpa John and Grandma Inez Theon. Grandma's real first name was Finis, however, she used Inez because she said Finis means finished, and "She wasn't finished yet." And as you will see she sure wasn't finished! Living right next door to us was Uncle Ed and Aunt Adeline with my cousins Harvel and Doris.

We attended Millgrove Bible Church every Wednesday for prayer meeting, Sunday morning for Sunday school followed by the church service. We also returned Sunday evening for testimonies, singing of hymns, and the pastor's challenging message. In Sunday school I learned songs like "The B-I-B-L-E, yes, that's the book for me, I stand alone on the word of God, the B-I-B-L-E", and "Jesus loves me, this I know, for the Bible tells me so."

During the church service the pastor would ask if anyone would like to give a testimony. Every Sunday night the same man, Pete Dutwieler, whose wife was my Sunday school teacher, would stand up and with his distinctive gravely voice, give praises of how God continued to bless and protect his family, and was always walking with them. It seems funny how we remember certain people's voices or mannerisms all our lives-I can still see and hear Pete.

After the Sunday morning service there were always families invited to our house for a fantastic feast, singing of hymns and Grandma playing the piano. She was an amazing piano player who often made her own compositions to the delight of everyone. After Grandma's concerts we had prayer followed by Uncle Ed reading passages from the Bible. The men would ponder and discuss the passages along with biblical prophecies and doctrines. While I didn't understand a lot of what was read and discussed, the atmosphere of church, feasts, music, prayer, and Bible reading resulted in wonderful feelings of happiness, security, and well-being. Life could not have been better.

Looking back now, I remember how the men would attempt to explain the many biblical predictions that defied our technology and understanding at the time. Events such as the antichrist being heard and seen around the world, the *Mark of the Beast*, a one-world government, cashless society, revived Roman Empire, and other prophesies they struggled to understand makes me realize how far we have journeyed toward those very events.

One prophecy they joyfully experienced being fulfilled before their eyes was the dry bones vision of Ezekiel, when in 1948 Israel became a nation again. In 1949 we couldn't imagine a computer or a World Wide Web, cable or satellite television, microchips, men walking on the moon, and most of all, credit or debit cards. It is amazing to me that in just over six brief decades, I have witnessed the development of the technology that sets the stage for every one of those prophesies to be fulfilled.

To emphasize just how far we have come, consider the following: In 1949 some people didn't have electric refrigerators and kept their perishables in "iceboxes." Every week the "iceman" would deliver large ice blocks that were put in the icebox to keep food cold. We had a "modern" bathroom with a flushing toilet, sink, and bathtub, however, many families in our neighborhood still had "outhouses." Outhouses were ancient versions of Port-A-Johns. They were usually erected quite a ways behind homes for obvious reasons. There were no sinks or flushing toilets, and all waste products piled up in the somewhat deep wooden box attached under a wooden board you sat on.

Outhouses were called "one," "two," or "three-holers", depending on how many toilet seats were cut into the board that served as a seat. Typically, the larger families had more seats because the mother of the family took all the children to the outhouse at once. There was no heat or light in outhouses and during the winter it was brutal. This resulted in the in-house use of ceramic bowls called "P-pots" that were emptied and washed each morning. We still have one of the "P-pots" which we now use as a flower planter.

In those days, there were no paper napkins, paper towels, or handy wipes. Instead, the "rag man" would go house to house selling old clothing, towels, and sheets that were used as cleaning rags. I remember visiting grandma's cousin Elijah, called "Lije," and his wife Lydia, whose house had no electricity. They used kerosene lamps for light and had a hand-dug well in the kitchen. Their water was accessed by a hand-pump mounted on a shelf attached to a cupboard that covered the well.

The pump had to be primed every time it was used and so a ceramic pitcher full of water was always left on the counter for that purpose. In many homes, including Lije and Lydia's, hot water for "washing up" or taking "sponge baths" came from water jackets that were part of woodstoves used for cooking and heat.

Remarkably, the house I purchased in 1975 still had one of those very multi-purpose wood-burning stoves. Most homes were built without insulation in the walls and had major cold air drafts. This resulted in most people wearing sweaters or thick long sleeved shirts over long underwear called "Long Johns," which were cotton one-piece body underwear. Quite often rooms in the houses were closed off for the winter and families would gather around "pot belly" wood burning stoves in their living rooms to keep warm. There was no heat in bedrooms, so thick "comforter" blankets and numerous wool quilts kept you warm in bed. Sometimes whole families slept in the same bed to keep warm during the cold country nights. At times it was hilarious when everyone would roll toward the heaviest person who, because of the weakness of the coil springs, would cause a deep valley in the bed.

There were no televisions and families would instead gather around gigantic wooden radios listening to the news, along with their favorite programs including: *Lights out, The Shadow, The Lone Ranger,* and *The Amos and Andy Show.* I remember what a thrill it was when we purchased our first television. Unlike today, televisions were only able to broadcast in black and white, color TV was not developed for many years. Our television had a round eight-inch screen with a prism mounted over the front to magnify the picture. The distortion was terrible and most of the time all that was displayed was a "test pattern."

The test pattern was a round logo with a standing Buffalo, the number "4," designating the station number, and a test sound which emitted the worst high pitched hum ever heard. The only TV programs I can remember are the news with Edward R. Murrow and the "Howdy Doody Show" with Buffalo Bob, Kookla, Fran, and Ollie, along with Princess Summer Fall Winter Spring. No one ever swore on radio or television, and every program had censors that screened the content before it could be aired.

Grandpa drove a Ford that was started by a crank mounted to the front of the engine; it had little heat and worse, no defroster. Because Dad worked at the Chevrolet plant, we drove a 1947 Chevy, the newest car in the neighborhood. Most of the roads were dirt and constantly full of ruts making the ride bumpy at best. When it rained cars were stuck everywhere, and in winter roads were often impassable.

As more and more families had telephones installed in their homes, a new plague emerged: *gossip*. Gossip was always in full bloom, however, telephones provided a means to gather more of it about more people, and pass it on faster. The telephone lines were connected to six or seven homes in what were known as "party lines." Operators in the telephone office would electronically ring a sequence of short or long rings alerting the family assigned that specific ring, that they had a call. Everyone on the party line would hear the rings and could pick up the phone to hear everyone else's conversations.

Our telephone number was 993, which meant that we were on the 99th party line and were alerted that we had a call by three short rings. Our neighbors the Webbers were given two short and one long ring. Once you identified everyone's ring, it was easy to get all the latest dirt on any given family. Sometimes everyone on the party line would listen in depending on the reputation of the family receiving the call. One benefit of the party lines and everyone listening to everyone else's conversations was that there was little need for psychologists and psychiatrists. The local "gossips" would bring your problems out into the open where they were dealt with and then left behind.

The one and only community doctor made house calls and dispensed medicine from his medical bag. Besides doing house calls, he delivered almost all of the children who were born in the local community. Many illnesses were treated with herbs and home remedies, for example, I still remember having to eat burnt toast covered with sugar and milk to cure intestinal ailments. When someone contracted a communicable disease the home was quarantined. The word, "Quarantine," was posted on the door with a warning that described what type of communicable disease was present.

Scores of people had died from typhoid fever and influenza in the 1920's and 30's so everyone was terrified of infectious diseases. Almost every child contracted mumps and measles and was quarantined. I remember being confined to a dark bedroom for 14 days with rubella, (German measles), and my face being swelled up with mumps. Polio left many young children paralyzed including my aunt Geraldine. People with respiratory diseases such as Tuberculosis, were put in "iron lungs" to help them breathe. The iron lungs were metal respirators enclosing the entire body except the patients head. The first time I saw one I was scared to death.

Busses and trains were the most popular means of transportation and the few airlines in existence flew propeller driven aircraft. During the past 50 years there have been more rapid social, technological, and medical advances than at anytime in recorded history. I can't even imagine what the men sitting in our living room discussing prophesy in 1949 would think if they were alive today. I do believe that they would be staring up in the sky looking for Jesus to return at any moment, I certainly am.

CHAPTER 2

FRIENDS, FAMILY, AND FOLLY

—ↄ␣w—

Every night I would cuddle up on Grandpa John's lap as he read the Buffalo Evening News or listened to the radio. I just adored him and felt so secure with his big strong arms gently holding me. After reading the newspaper or listening to the world news on the radio, we would dig out my favorite books, "The Armadillo and the Monkey" and "The Wizard of OZ," which I made him read at least three times every night. However, what captivated me the most were his exciting stories about working on the railroad and serving his country during the Spanish-American War.

There were stories of his friend "Skinny Long" who he laughingly said was, "Actually very short." Skinny was killed when a conductor yelled, "Look out," and Skinny stuck his head out the railroad car to see what to look out for only to have his head caught on a mail retrieval hook. Other exciting stories included runaway trains that went careening off the tracks and crashed, and how God had protected Grandpa from being crushed between two railroad cars. I remember thinking that God must be very strong to reach down from Heaven and hold those two cars apart just so Grandpa wouldn't get hurt.

Grandpa John served in the Army from 1898 to 1901 during the Spanish-American War. He was stationed in the Philippine Islands and, except for contracting malaria which plagued him the rest of his life, loved it there. He always said he enjoyed the warm weather, tropical fruit, and beautiful jungle-covered mountains, and was sure that I would like it there. He didn't realize how prophetic his words were as I indeed loved the Philippines when I was stationed there from 1966 to 1968 during the Vietnam War.

Grandpa was extremely proud that he was chosen to be his military outfit's Company Artificer, which is the term for military mechanic. He also complained about the men in his Company who were always trying to borrow money from him to gamble and buy, "Their damned old beer." He could not fathom wasting his hard earned money on any vice, especially gambling, alcohol, and cigarettes.

Every morning Grandpa would get up at 6 a.m. sharp, empty his "P-pot," wash and shave, then make his bowl of oatmeal, blessing the meal by reciting the Lord's Prayer in German and English. One constant each day besides his oatmeal, Lord's Prayer, and singing of German songs to me, was his daily advice. He repeatedly warned, "Bobby, always do good and tell the truth or you will go down the slippery slide," which was his description of how and where bad people and liars went at their death, down the slippery slide to Hell! He also told me to work hard and make sure I paid my bills because if I didn't pay my bills they would throw me in the "Poor House." It wasn't until years later that I discovered that there was a debtor's prison nicknamed, "The Poor House." Hmmm, a debtor's prison, *that* would be an interesting concept today.

I loved to be with Grandpa so much that one time when he climbed onto the roof to complete some shingle repairs, I followed him right up the ladder. The problem was that he didn't realize that I was up there standing precariously close to the edge. One of our neighbors watched the entire scene develop from her kitchen window and was sure that at any moment I would plunge to my death.

She ran over to our house and summoning as much composure as possible softly alerted Grandpa that his four year old grandson was standing behind him inches from the edge of the roof. He calmly turned and said, "Bobby, come up here and help Grandpa," which I gladly did. He hugged me and with his big hand on mine, helped me hammer a roofing nail in. By then everyone in our family was out on the lawn applauding as he carried me down the ladder. Although he was in his mid-seventies he was still a mountain of a man as strong as could be with a rock solid constitution.

Grandpa John and Grandma Finis always seemed to be at odds. I fondly remember the times when gram would go to visit the neighbors and he would say, "Is she out of sight?" I would run to look out the window and as soon as I couldn't see her I would scurry to get the waffle maker out of the cupboard. We would chow down on buttermilk waffles covered with mounds of home-churned butter and maple syrup. Grandpa would say "Dasn't say anything," which was his favorite expression for better not say anything about eating waffles when Grandma came home or we would get skinned alive. Of course she always smelled the sweet aroma of the maple syrup and scolded us saying that the waffles would spoil our supper. However, Grandpa and I didn't care if supper was ruined because those waffles were just fabulous.

When I wasn't gallivanting all over western New York with Grandma Finis or following Grandpa John as he worked around the homestead, I would be playing school with my cousin Doris and the kids in our neighborhood. Doris was the teacher and we were the students, and although I took it as a game, she took school very seriously. Consequently, at times Doris the teacher also became the principal as well as truant officer.

She taught us math, reading, and spelling, drilling them into our heads with repetition and tests. Although she allowed the neighborhood kids a little slack, she wasn't satisfied until I scored 100% on every test. Of course she always had incentives and rewards attached to achievement. She proudly fancied herself as a super teacher and often let everyone know it. I really enjoyed being with Doris whether I was in her classes or just at play and the impact she had on my life is still evident after all these years.

Having a wealth of relatives living in close proximity to each other on the family homestead had many advantages including the security of built-in baby sitters and playmates that were your cousins. However, drawbacks such as family members gladly telling on you when you did something wrong were all too common. We were never able to keep secrets because one of the cousins would slip up and, bingo, there went all our plans. It also meant that little ears with big mouths often overheard adult family secrets. And so it was when Doris dropped the bomb. "Bobby, Aunt Gert and Uncle John are not your real Mommy and Daddy! Your Mom didn't bore you, you were adopted."

I ran to Momma as fast as I could stammering, "You didn't bore me?" I can still see the tears in her eyes as she put me on her lap with her arms hugging me so very tightly and with her voice cracking, explained that she couldn't have babies so God sent me to her. I remember thinking that if God sent me to her, where did he keep me before he sent me to Mommy and Daddy? She told me that I was very special because I was adopted and for the next few weeks everyone kept telling me that I was special. However, something in my little mind sensed that maybe I was *different, not special* because of it. I was a little worried that maybe if I was bad Momma might be able to send me back to God!

The security and trust of a close-knit family, along with the wonderful church services followed by the Sunday afternoon music, feasts, and Bible study helped the shock of discovering my adoption wear off. It wasn't very long before everything got back to normal. I would be in "Doris School," follow Gramps around, or go gallivanting with Gram. Little did I realize that my Heaven of a world was about to end and heartache come roaring in like a lion.

One day out of the clear blue sky Dad took me for a ride to meet a friend of his named Eunice. I had never met her before but she seemed like a nice lady and I immediately hit it off with her two children who were about the same age as I was. We played with their toys and games and I even got to pretend I was Doris the teacher when we played school. It didn't take long to figure out why Doris enjoyed being the teacher, the teacher runs the class and the students do what the teacher tells them. It was a new experience to be in charge but I kind of liked it.

Over the next few months we visited Eunice and her children quite a few times. Then something very strange happened, Dad asked me if I would like to have Eunice's children as my new brother and sister. It sounded great, just like that I was going to have a brother and sister to bring to our home. Wow, Mom would be so happy, she couldn't have children but God sent me to her, and now Dad and I were bringing her two more. Doris would have two more students for school and I just knew they would love all our weekend festivities. I wasn't quite sure how Eunice was going to fit in but it seemed she would become an aunt just like Aunt Adeline.

Well, we didn't bring the new brother and sister or aunt home, in fact, after we got home Dad packed up and moved out. I didn't understand it, but somehow, Mom and Dad didn't love each other anymore and within a short time they were in court fighting over who was going to have custody of me. After that, Dad only got to see me two weekends a month. When he picked me up for "his weekend" we went to Eunice's house. I still enjoyed playing with her kids and Eunice was nice but I became confused and scared when Dad asked if I would like to move out west where Eunice would become my new mom and her children my new brother and sister. When I told Mom what Dad had asked me she started screaming and crying, yelling that John would never see me again! Those were prophetic words because the next time Dad came to pick me up for his weekend visit Grandpa hid me in the cellar of our house.

Even now I can vividly replay that Saturday in my mind. Our basement had a dirt floor and was muddy so we had to walk on narrow planks to get to the corner where Grandpa could look out a small window to see if Dad was going to come to the door of our house to try to take me. On all other visits Dad pulled into the driveway and blew the car horn twice as a signal for Mom to send me out to his car. However, as Dad repeatedly blew the horn Grandpa said to me, "Bobby, you are not going with him anymore." After about ten minutes as Dad slowly backed out of our driveway, Grandpa held me up so I could get a last glimpse of him.

I didn't see Daddy John again until I was 18 years old and only three more times the rest of his life. He never paid a penny of the support ordered by the court, and moved back to New York only when I was over the age where he would have to shell out any money for me. In 2005 I accidentally came face to face with Eunice, and as my mind was flooded with the pain, and anguish she caused by breaking up our family, a battle instantly raged in my soul. Here at last was my chance to exact some revenge, I could tear this home wrecking Jezebel apart. As I was torn between vengeance, retribution, and mercy, God gave me His grace and I was able to forgive her. His amazing grace also allowed and guided me to even help her get tires for her car. Whew! Thank you, Jesus!

CHAPTER 3

CULTURE SHOCK

—ɯ—

Grandpa John had two extremely strong traits; stub-bornness and independence. When Uncle Ed sold his house and Grandma let him and his family move in with us, Grandpa balked at the idea and moved out. Although he was nearly 80 years old, he caught a ride to Florida with a man he knew who was moving there, bought land next to an orange grove, and began building himself a small house. When he finally sent a letter home it was to let us know that he was now living in Lakeland, Florida, and that he was never returning to New York.

He also informed Grandma that she could join him if she felt like it. When Gram did go to see him in Florida, she never stayed more than a month to two before returning to New York. Just before she left Florida she would bake dozens of chocolate chip cookies which Grandpa would try to ration until she returned. The only letters Grandma would receive from him would say, "Getting low on cookies when you coming back? John."

With Dad and Grandpa now gone, and Uncle Ed, Aunt Adeline, Doris, and Harvel, now living in the homestead, I was sent off to live with my mother's other sister Aunt Gerry, and her family in Eden, New York. Mom went to live and work in Buffalo only coming to see me on weekends. She didn't have a car so she would take the *Blue Bus* from Buffalo to Eden. I remember waiting for the bus in joyous anticipation of seeing her. She would always say she wasn't going to cry and then burst into tears, bawling her eyes out every time I would run to greet her with a big hug and kisses. I would beg her, "Please Mommy don't cry," her tears hurt me as much as they hurt her. My wonderful, sheltered world was rapidly disintegrating into a broken shell of insecurity, confusion, and pain.

Living with Aunt Gerry and Uncle Howard Roeller, along with my cousins, Johnny and Richard, was quite a shocking experience. They never went to church and there definitely wasn't any Sunday afternoon feast, music, and Bible study. They owned Roeller's Hotel which had people living in its rented rooms, served daily lunch and dinner, and was also the number one watering hole for local drunks. While we lived in their house just around the corner, we spent the majority of our time at the hotel.

Life there was exciting and fast paced with the hustle and bustle of preparing the meals, cleaning the rented rooms, restocking the bar, and interacting with the people who daily frequented the barroom. The men were always telling vile stories and jokes, most of which contained swearing, and sexual overtones that were new, different, and shocking to my ears and mind. However, the majority of the patrons in the barroom roared with laughter at them.

Looking back now I realize how easy it was to become seduced by the whole vile atmosphere and see it as exciting and rewarding. The men and women who drank their lives away in that barroom received their identity from their fellow drunks. As alcohol numbed their senses and lowered their inhibitions, they were able to act out their pain, anguish, and fears in this artificial, socially acceptable environment.

That environment also included acting out aggression through fights, both verbal and physical. I remember a very thin, small man named Joe, who, when sober, was quiet and nice. However, when he would drink, became extremely boisterous, vile, and aggressive. Everyone in the barroom would just ignore his tirades, letting him act as if he was a "tough guy," all the time knowing that he couldn't physically intimidate anyone.

There was also a lady who was the picture of conservative virtue when she was sober. However, when drinking, lost all control and became a Jezebel, acting like a harlot. Most of the men that frequented Roeller's Hotel would give my cousin Johnny and me quarters for the jukebox, or to play the bowling and pinball machines. Uncle Howard, who was at the hotel every minute it was open cleaning or tending the bar, would let us eat pretzels, potato chips, pickled eggs, and sausage anytime we wanted them.

On Sundays we never went to church but instead cleaned the hotel. Johnny and I loved to sweep and mop the floor in the barroom because we would find coins that the drunks had dropped. Sometimes we would hit the jackpot and find a five or ten dollar bill. Because of what were then known as the "Blue Laws," bars in hotels couldn't open until after 4 p.m. on Sunday, so we had plenty of time to clean the place up before the rat race started again.

Aunt Gerry and Uncle Howard owned two horses named Sim and Lucky. After we cleaned the barroom Johnny and I would pack a lunch and go horseback riding in the hills and wooded areas surrounding the Village of Eden. He taught me how to trap fox and hunt raccoon. However, the most interesting thing Johnny taught me was the difference between boys and girls in his "anatomy class," held in a small patch of trees behind the hotel.

Classroom instruction included Johnny, who, as the teacher, talked two neighborhood girls into taking off all their clothes to let us "inspect" their bodies, and pointed out all the specifics of the female anatomy. While Johnny was an honor roll anatomy scholar, his command of academics was quite poor and he failed several grades more than once. He was finally sent to live with Grandpa in Florida, to finish 11th and 12th grade. And while Johnny was able to complete high school at Lakeland High, he didn't seem to learn much about people or race relations because he joined the Ku Klux Klan. I guess he thought that by attacking people solely because of their race he could somehow lift himself above them.

While Johnny had a hard time with school, his brother Richard was the epitome of academic achievement, graduating as valedictorian of his class. He was an intense person with an extremely strong and opinionated personality. Often patronizing, arrogant, and sarcastic, Richard dominated any and all conversations. He belittled anyone who dared to disagree with him and seemed almost sadistic. His social circle was narrow and he often bragged that his close friends were from the richest and most influential families in Buffalo.

Richard eventually became a Buffalo Evening News press photographer. He received many awards for excellence in his craft, and many of his pictures were published in prestigious magazines. Richard drove sports cars and owned vintage Ford Thunderbirds and Chevrolet Corvettes. He had women swooning over him and the means to purchase almost any worldly luxury he desired. However, he never seemed happy and I always thought there was something secret and strange hidden within him. In later years he became a blatant homosexual, president of the Western New York Gay Society, and extremely dedicated to the militant homosexual group "ACT UP." In the early 1990's Richard died of AIDS.

Because I started school while living with Aunt Gerry and Uncle Howard, who were always at the hotel, Grandma came to live with us to take care of me when I came home from school. This had two effects: first, I spent much less time at the hotel and second, I was again brought under the strong Christian influence of my Grandmother. Before she sent me off to school, she read Bible passages and prayed for me, my classmates, and our teacher.

If Mom wasn't coming to visit me on weekends, Gram and I would go gallivanting all over western New York, visiting her friends. When school was closed for the Christmas and Easter holidays we would jump on the train and go to Florida to visit Grandpa. Because Grandpa was retired form the Erie Lackawanna Railroad, we had Gold Passes that allowed us to ride the railroad anywhere in the United States free of charge.

In Florida I had a great time playing with the kids in the neighborhood. There were railroad tracks across the street from my Grandfather's house, and my friends and I would go along the tracks looking for Coral snakes. Coral snakes have extremely toxic venom that would surely have killed us if we were bit by one. Grandma was always chasing us away from the tracks and told us that if she caught us playing on the tracks we wouldn't have to worry about being bit by a Coral snake, because she would "skin us alive!" Sometimes Grandma was more toxic than the snakes.

Another adventure that we really enjoyed was to go down the tracks to a spot where hobos would jump off the trains. The hobos would camp under two large trees covered with Spanish moss. After a few days stay, they would jump a train heading in a different direction. Calling the area under the trees "Grand Central Station," there were usually two or three of them sleeping in a pile of the moss beneath the twin trees.

Some people in our neighborhood warned us that the hobos sometimes did terrible things to children. While the warnings did scare us, they never kept us from going to listen to their exciting stories of riding the trains across America.

The hobos always had a small fire burning to heat coffee, which they drank out of tin cans. While their hygiene wasn't the best and sleeping in that Spanish moss in 90-plus degree heat didn't help their body odors, we still liked to be around them. They would politely ask if we had any spare change, prompting us to scrounge up as much money as we could, to give to them. They would pool the panhandled money and go up to the corner store to buy a bottle of the cheapest wine available. They always asked us if we wanted a "swig" from the community wine bottle as they passed it around their campfire. However, not one of us ever took them up on the invitation.

Some people would drop off cans of soup or beans for them. Many of the hobos cried as they talked about their families and how they had been on the road trying to find work but just somehow never went back home. Every few days hobos would hop a train and leave as new ones jumped off other trains. As the new arrivals got situated, we would check to see if we knew any of them. Every now and then, one or two that we knew would return and we couldn't wait to hear about their travels. Occasionally, we would receive the sad news about a hobo we knew who had died jumping a train or in a fight.

The two boys living across the street were my best buddies, I could relate to their situation, their father was gone and their mother had to work to support them. This left a lot of time for us to play and explore the railroad tracks, the hobo camp, or the vast orange groves behind Grandpa's house. It was hard saying goodbye to my friends in Florida when the school vacations were over and Gram and I had to return to New York.

We would write letters to each other for awhile, but then get caught up in our separate lives and stop writing. Within five years they had moved and I seldom went to Florida. I found out two years ago that one of those boys did alright for himself; he started an automobile parts store that became a franchise across America: good for him.

During the summer months when I was out of school, Gram and I traveled all over western New York visiting friends. She was an extremely altruistic person who helped any and everyone she met. If there was a neighborhood family in need, there was Gram doing whatever it took to meet the need. When smallpox, influenza, and other epidemics ravaged the country in the early 20th century, Gram tended the sick and buried the dead, which included her own son. She delivered scores of babies and even delivered her own four children. Superman had nothing on Grandma!

Although she stood less than five feet tall and weighed a mere 80 pounds, she was a giant of a woman with a constitution as strong as tempered steel and a will to match. Gram was up well before dawn reading her Bible, a practice she continued throughout her entire 89 years on earth. She memorized so many verses that everyone called her the "Walking Bible Encyclopedia." She instantly had verses to speak into any need or situation and was a mighty prayer warrior.

Her reputation as a Christian giant with amazing gifts was legendary throughout western New York. People would write letters asking her to pray for their health, healing, and families. If someone lost their wedding ring, jewelry, or any other precious item, there they would be at our door asking Gram to pray, so they could find the lost item. Gram would open her Bible and meditate on "God's Word," then pray for the specific items. The next morning she would tell the person to look in a specific area, where, sure enough, they would find the lost items.

At times she would be overcome with a need to sit down and go into deep prayer. When this happened she would receive visions. On one occasion she was in Buffalo visiting friends when she received a vision of her mother's home burning and her mom running out of the house with severe burns to her arms. She also saw her struggling with firemen, as she tried to run back into the house to open her piano bench. Gram immediately returned home to find the house in flames and her Mother being treated for severe burns to her forearms. The reason for her severe burns was her repeated attempts to enter the house to retrieve her beloved music scores from her piano bench! I must admit that her visions kind of freaked me out at times and I was glad she didn't receive them very often.

Like her mother, Gram loved to play the piano. She practiced almost every day, composing songs as she played. Even now as I remember her playing the piano, my mind flashes back to the wonderful Sundays after church with the whole family together at the homestead. It was truly a taste of Heaven.

One thing I knew for sure, when Gram said, "Bobby, get some clothes packed, we are going out for a day or two," I was about to embark on an adventure going who knew where and doing who knew what. Going out for a day or two with Gram was like going out with Huckleberry Finn and Tom Sawyer.

Because she was so compassionate we often ended up at wakes. Gram could never, "Pass up people at their most needy time." In the 1950's most rural families laid out their deceased loved one in the living rooms of their homes which were called parlors. Homes that had deceased family members laid out in their parlors also placed a black wreath on their door. Consequently, when the first commercial funeral homes opened they followed suit and were called "Funeral Parlors," displaying black wreaths on their doors as well.

And so it was when Gram saw a house with a black wreath on its door, she boldly let the love of God lead her into the home of the grieving family where she would mourn with and comfort them. It was irrelevant to her that she never knew the family or the deceased. Making things more interesting was that if she knew the family, she would pitch right in and prepare meals. She would clean the house and even, much to my chagrin, powder the deceased's face, so, as she put it, "They don't look so dead."

Often we ended up staying at the house for the two days the body was being shown before the funeral. Gram and I would often sleep on the couch right in the parlor along side the casket. She would be fast asleep snoring away in ten minutes, however, I didn't sleep at all, keeping one eye on the corpse the entire night. During those long hours of darkness, I was sure the eyes opened or a hand moved.

Gram struggled with many afflictions including asthma, bleeding ulcers, and often contracted pneumonia. However, the maladies never kept her from being her cantankerous stubborn self, especially when it came to her appearance. For example, she put her hair, "Up in rags," every night. This was a process where rags were cut into small strips and she pulled her hair into many clusters and tied the rags around each of them. The result was that when she untied the rags in the morning her hair would be curly.

Gram was so stubborn that when she suffered bleeding from stomach ulcers so severe she had to be rushed to the hospital for emergency surgery, she refused to be taken into the ambulance until she had tied her hair up in rags. When the surgery was completed, the surgeon informed us that he had to remove four fifths of her stomach. His prognosis was that her chances of survival were slim at best.

He also told us we should get her things in order. Get her things in order, ha! Three weeks after the surgery she was at home scrubbing the floors. In fact, Gram attended that same surgeon's funeral a decade later. Some of the benefits of having Gram stay at your house were that if you removed a shirt or any other piece of clothing, before you could retrieve it, she had washed it. She also washed the bedding every other day, and was always ready to cook a meal for you, no matter what time it was.

Gram did have a few quirks that you had to get used to if she came to visit. She had a pet mud turtle named Heady. She found Heady in the road one day as she was walking to a neighbor's house and grew so attached to it that for the next ten years, where Gram went, so went Heady. She kept Heady in a small shoe box. Over the years she and that turtle became soul mates and were inseparable. Gram was the only person in the world who was able to train a mud turtle to follow commands. It is hard to believe and if I hadn't experienced it first hand, I wouldn't have believed it myself, but she did train that turtle.

When Gram would get up in the predawn hours, she washed him and let him out of his box. The turtle would follow her into the kitchen and over to the refrigerator, where Gram would get raw hamburger to feed him. Gram would say "Ok Heady back to your box," and away he would go back to the living room scratching the side of his box until Gram put him and his breakfast into it. At times Gram would let Heady explore the area surrounding the house and all she had to do when she wanted him, was call his name and sure enough he came right back to her.

Another of her passions, besides reading her Bible continuously from cover to cover and daily hours of prayer, was saving newspaper articles. As she read the Buffalo Evening News, she always had a pair of scissors ready to cut out "her articles." When she died there was literally a room at my mother's apartment completely filled with boxes of newspaper articles. I only wish I would have kept some of them which dated back to the early 1900s.

Gram was so headstrong and determined that she even chose when she would die. When my wife became pregnant with our second child Gram was 89 years old and in extremely poor health. However, she declared she would hold the baby in her arms before she died. When my wife went beyond her due date, Gram informed her that she better have the child soon because she was already dead but only hanging on to hold the baby. Much to Grandma's chagrin, my wife went another two weeks before our daughter Jennifer's birth. Sure enough within days after holding Jennifer Gram breathed her last. I'm sure she heard God say, "Well done my good and faithful servant."

CHAPTER 4

A SECOND CHANCE

—ⵑⵑⵡ—

J ust about the time I had come to grips with the reality that
my life was now going to be full of instability, insecurity,
and constant change, Mom informed me that she was going
to marry Charles Alexander. Charlie, as he liked to be called,
lived in Corfu, New York, and we would be moving into
his home. He had two sons, Jack who was in the Army and
Ed who was fourteen-years-old. Charlie's wife Wanda had
recently died, and it seemed to be perfect match. He wanted
a wife and mother for Ed, and mom desperately wanted
a father for me. It seemed a little strange that I only met
Charlie twice and the next thing I knew we were on a vacation in Atlantic City, celebrating their marriage.

Memories of the wonderful life I had known on the homestead flooded my mind. I envisioned our new family going to
church, people coming to our house for a feast, gram playing
the piano, followed by Bible study and prayer. I wondered
where Charlie and Ed went to church and if there was a man
like Pete Dutweiler from Millgrove in their church. With
great anticipation I waited for that first Sunday and the return
of stability and security to my life. It seemed even better than
I could ever have imagined, I was going to have a new dad,
new home, and two new brothers.

I can vividly remember the very day we moved into Charlie's house and I was told that from that day on my name would be Robert Alexander. I also recall thinking that if daddy John Faulring didn't want or love me anymore, it was good to have a new dad and his last name. What I didn't know was that Charlie didn't adopt me, so therefore my legal name remained Robert Faulring. When they registered me for school Dad told the secretary that my name was Robert Alexander. I really liked the name Alexander because Dad told me that he was related to Alexander the Great. I didn't know a thing about Alexander the Great, however at that point in my life, anything great attached to me, sounded like Heaven.

Well, Sunday came and I experienced the proverbial bursting of my envisioned bubble. Dad did not attend church, ever, and now neither did mom. There was no feast, music, Bible study, or prayer, and, in fact, Charlie openly mocked the Bible and Christians. He said things like "Jesus was a whoremonger" and "You don't know if Jesus was crucified or shot off a jackass!" Yikes, that sounded dreadfully like those drunks in the barroom at Uncle Howard's hotel. I also vividly remember Charlie throwing the Bible out of our kitchen window during a rain storm and saying, "If God is real, let him throw it back in."

However, as twisted as it was, on occasion Dad and Mom would tell Ed and me that we had to attend the local community church. When those occasions came along, Ed and I would walk or ride Ed's bicycle the two-miles to the church. We also would pack play clothes and food in a bag, and as soon as the church service was over, we would high tail it for the refuge of the wooded area that was on our way home. Our friends Bruce and Homer Fisher would leave clues in the woods that would lead us to where they were hiding. It was exciting to follow all the signs and then finally rendezvous with them at one of our camps where we would share the experience of the chase, over hot dogs and Kool Aid.

Ed and I also had a 1952 version of a go-cart. We constructed it by nailing two by fours together to make a wooden frame which we attached to a wagon axle, then nailed an old washtub on to the frame to make it into a go-cart. We attached it to our walk-behind garden tractor and named the contraption, "Tonka." It was our chariot and we traveled the neighborhood acting as if we were gladiators in the Coliseum. We would also ride Tonka the two-miles to Hamilton's farm where we swam in their pond which had a raft anchored in the middle. I couldn't swim a lick but trusted Ed completely as he swam all around the pond with me clinging to his back.

One afternoon Ed put me on the raft and told me to jump in and he would catch me. I leaped into the water and Ed was there to grab me before I went under. I thought it was the greatest feat I could accomplish and begged him to let me jump off the raft again. Ed nodded with a broad smile, but suddenly his expression changed and he yelled, "I'm being pulled under."

At first I thought he was kidding and just trying to scare me, however, the look on his face told a different story. Ed was struggling to keep his head above the water and losing the battle. He looked directly into my eyes as he was being pulled under the water for the third time and gulped the one word I didn't want to hear; "Help!"

As I frantically screamed for help, Ed went under the water and didn't come up. I was so scared and felt so helpless looking off the edge of the raft, knowing that Ed was drowning and I couldn't do anything to save him. In desperation, I laid flat on my stomach on the raft and held my arms down in the water, hoping that he would be able to grab them and pull himself up. In abject horror, I rolled myself into a fetal position thinking that Ed had drowned when up he suddenly popped on the other side of the raft gulping for air.

Apparently, the cable that attached the raft to a large concrete slab on the bottom of the pond had wrapped around Ed's leg. As the raft moved back and forth it pulled him under the water. Thankfully, he kept his cool and when he was dragged down the third time, swam toward the bottom, and got his leg free. As Ed sat on that raft and hugged me, I felt a special bond develop, one that you can only experience but not describe. To prevent me from developing a fear of going into the water, Ed made me ride on his back as he swam all around the pond.

Ed had another passion, playing basketball. We had a basketball backboard and hoop attached to an old apple tree behind our house. Ed practiced dribbling and shooting baskets almost everyday. His specialty was the two hand set shot and he practiced shooting it over and over. In high school Ed was the star of the basketball team. He could out dribble everyone and was a master at stealing the ball from the opposing team. Besides being the star of the basketball team, he was also the quarterback of the school football team.

Because Dad worked swing shifts, he only attended a few of Ed's games and mom never any at all. In fact, during Ed's, and later my, entire high school years, Mom never attended even one of our sporting events and dad only made a few. While the lack of attention to our sporting events hurt us emotionally, there was a silver lining in the apathy; it also applied to our academic performance. They never attended parent/teacher conferences, nor answered requests from educators to meet with them to discuss our academic progress or lack there of.

This had two effects; it drove Ed and me closer because we received our reinforcement from each other and our peers, and also gave us an open invitation to do almost anything we desired. Ed was very mature and responsible, so we seldom ended up in any real trouble. I loved Ed and the security I enjoyed with him being my big brother. We had the heartache of parents that constantly worked with little time for nurturing and guiding us, but the Heaven of our lives together. I made a vow that when I grew up I was going to be just like my big brother, Ed.

The secure life I enjoyed with Ed came to a screeching halt after his junior year when he quit school and joined the United States Army. I was crushed and felt abandoned again. Because Mom worked the day shift at the Sylvania Television Plant and dad the swing shift at Chevrolet in Buffalo, I was left to get myself up, wash, dress, and make my own breakfast before school. Thank God, Gram often came to stay with us. She got me up, cooked a great breakfast, and sent me off to school with a prayer.

When I returned home from school there was Gram reading her Bible, after washing all the clothes I left laying around, vacuuming the rugs, scrubbing our floors, and cooking a great dinner that would be simmering on the stove. Dad would kid mom, saying that he should have married Gram, instead of her.

During the three-years Ed was in the Army, my older brother Jack, who drove commercial trucks, tried to pick up some of the slack by taking me along on his trips. We would sleep in his truck, me on the floor and Jack on the seat. Jack ended up quitting truck driving and aimlessly drifted in and out of many menial jobs, never staying at any of them very long.

What Jack really liked to do was skip work and go fishing, which fit right into my train of thought. There was nothing better than skipping school to go fishing with Jack. He was an extremely large, strong man, however, he certainly wasn't going to be hired to be a brain surgeon. He quit school in the 10th grade joining the Army. Unfortunately, his Army career was cut short when he was court marshaled and dishonorably discharged for stealing a car and being involved in a barroom brawl. He was easily caught because he parked the stolen car in front of the place.

Jack had no idea who Jesus was, except to use his name in vain, which was his habit. He never attended church and didn't like those who did. On top of that, he felt that all ministers were hypocrites only trying to scam people out of their money. Jack had better use for his money, like buying a fishing boat, tackle, cigars, beer, and hard cider. When we would go on our fishing jaunts, he would sing profane songs and tell vile stories.

He didn't take any guff from anyone, letting people know the disdain he felt towards them in no uncertain insulting terms, which always included colorful adjectives and vivid metaphors. Mom and Jack never seemed to see eye-to-eye on any matter. Mom often tried to persuade me not to go with Jack, however, we would hightail it out fishing as soon as she left for work.

Jack was *loster than lost*, and I would never dream that he could or would come to Jesus Christ. God is so very good. Jack had left New York in the mid 1970's, moving to Tampa, Florida where Dad bought him a small house. Then for a few years Jack just disappeared. Dad finally received a letter from him saying that he had moved to Val Dosta, Georgia, and was, "Working on a road crew." We then lost track of Jack again and were unable to contact him for over two years. Dad sent many letters that were all returned as undeliverable with no forwarding address.

In 1976 I was going to Florida for a vacation and Dad asked if I would try to locate Jack and see if he was still in Val Dosta. I spent two fruitless days trying to track Jack down. Then just when I was about to give up, I accidentally ran into a man who worked for the State of Georgia Highway Department that knew Jack. He sent me to the main office of the Highway Department, and sure enough, Jack was working that very day. The Highway Superintendent escorted me to the job site where Jack was operating a bucket loader.

As I approached the loader, Jack strained to see who was coming toward him. When he realized it was me, he vaulted off that loader and gave me a bear hug that I was sure was going to crush me. Jack's boss gave him the rest of the day off which we spent in his mobile home. I was astonished to find that there was no beer or other type of alcoholic beverage in Jack's refrigerator. And to my amazement, right where I pictured he would have been sitting drinking a cold one, there sat a Bible! Jack told me that he was now a Christian, attending church and prayer meetings regularly.

You could have knocked me over with a feather. He also said that he was getting married in two weeks and that his wife to be was a wonderful Christian woman. What I didn't realize was that God had orchestrated my vacation and hunt for Jack because he wanted me to know that my brother was saved. Two days before the wedding, Jack was killed while operating that same loader I first saw him on. We buried him in his wedding suit. Jack, Praise God, the next time I find you, it will be in Heaven.

CHAPTER 5

THE PLOT THINS OUT

—∭—

E d was gone and I could only be with Jack on a limited
basis, so I started to pal around with the two other boys
my age that lived next door to us. Bruce Fisher was a year
younger than I, while Dale Stone was a year older. Dale was
a big strong kid who could and did beat the daylights out of
me on occasion. Dale's family would have fit perfectly in the
Andy of Mayberry television program. His Dad, Al, worked
at a local car repair shop, while his Mother Eva, was home
taking care of the one daughter and two other sons in their
family.

The Stone family was poor for quite some time and lived
in a broken down house that had been handed down from
generation to generation. They still had an outhouse long
after everyone in the neighborhood had indoor bathrooms.
Al raised cows to supply milk and bulls for meat. They also
raised pigs and chickens, some for meat and some that were
sold to cover the cost of raising the animals.

It was exciting, grisly, and scary when it came time to
slaughter the animals. Dale, Bruce, and I would climb up
into the hay loft in the barn to get a bird's eye view of the
process. The man who slaughtered the bulls would shoot
them right between the eyes and then cut them wide open

to remove their inner parts. He took pleasure in cutting the hearts out and tossing them up in the loft at us. We would squeal in excitement and fear as we scrambled to keep the steaming hearts from hitting us.

Watching a pig's death was downright amazing and somewhat sickening. Their back feet were bound with rope, followed by the squirming creatures being hoisted up in the air by block and tackle, where their throats were then cut. The pigs squealed in agony as they bled to death.

It was actually kind of humorous, in a twisted sort of way, to watch the chicken's fate. They were held in a position so their necks were across a log and then their heads were chopped off. What was funny was that as soon as the deed was done, the headless fowl ran all around the yard flapping their wings until they bled to death.

I spent a lot of time at the Stone's house, usually after school until Mom got home from work. Dale's mother Eva would make us soup and sandwiches before we ran off to play. Living in a small, primarily rural farming community, we seldom had more than four other kids to play with. Our baseball and basketball games were usually three against three. The Stones were a close knit family and enjoyed sitting on their porch together, talking, and watching the sunset.

Their big family event, which took place once every three months, involved loading the family into their 1953 Kiser Frazier automobile, and driving the 12 miles to the Dipson Theater in the city of Batavia to see a movie. Dale was often allowed to bring me long as his guest. I look back now with such fond memories of eating popcorn, Cracker Jacks, and Milk Duds while watching those corny Ma and Pa Kettle movies with the Stone family. And like a bridge across time I can still feel the longing I had for a close, loving, and secure family like theirs. When Mom wasn't working she pursued her favorite pastime, shopping. She would buy me anything my heart desired and loved to get my picture taken at the best photo studios. On top of that, my clothes were always purchased at the most expensive stores in Buffalo.

When the school sent a note home informing Mom that eye tests revealed I needed glasses for reading, she took me to the highest priced optometrist and purchased the most expensive frames for the glasses. When I tried out my glasses, Dad jokingly called me "Four-eyes." That was the end of the eyewear, I found them a new home in the garbage can refusing to let Mom get me another pair.

What was interesting is that I was never punished for throwing the glasses away. Amazingly, my eyes must have healed themselves because when I enlisted in the military 13 years later, my vision was a perfect 20/20. I didn't have to wear another pair of glasses until I was over 30 years old. Kind of makes you wonder doesn't it?

Because of the guilt Mom felt due to adopting me and then having Daddy John abandon us, it was easy to manipulate her into buying me anything I wanted or letting me do anything I desired. The result was that she was turning me into a spoiled brat. Dad pointed out that I needed discipline and tried to invoke some consequences for my spoiled behavior. However, Mom would have none of it and indulged my every whim. What she didn't see was that down inside, I really desired the security of the limits and punishment that Dad knew I deserved and needed. Mom also hated it when Dad would say "Spare the rod and spoil the child," and "Gert you're wrecking a good child."One thing about mom that was really interesting was her driving abilities or should I say lack of them. Her escapades behind the wheel are legendary to this very day. I will share a few of the volumes of stories about her being behind the wheel of an automobile.

It all started back in 1952 when she decided to buy a new Pontiac to "Drive back and forth to work and the store." There were problems right from the get-go at the car dealership. In those days most of the cars had manual transmissions, which meant that in order to properly place the vehicle in motion, the driver had to be able to walk and chew gum at the same time; an attribute Mom lacked. She just couldn't coordinate the fine art of putting the clutch in before shifting into first gear and gently releasing it while applying a little pressure on the gas peddle to start the car in motion.

Four things stand out in my mind about that first ride with her. First, that terrible grinding sound; second, how many times I flew against the dashboard; third, how the engine roared at 40 miles-per-hour in first gear; and finally, the screams and swearing from Dad as Mom plowed into the back of his Buick to stop her car. But it got better! In 1952 you could buy a car, drive awhile, and then get your drivers license. And now that Mom had purchased a car, she decided it was time to take her road test and get her license.

I recall that process almost as vividly as the first ride home. It was a beautiful Monday morning as we pulled up to the Department of Motor Vehicles testing site and got in line for the road test. Mom watched intently as the DMV examiner, dressed in his dark blue uniform with clipboard in hand, walked up to each car. He asked the driver a number of questions recording their responses on his clipboard, then entered the vehicle on the passenger's side and away went the cars. In approximately ten minutes the car returned to the test site. Then the tester told the driver whether they passed or failed and got out of the car, proceeding to the next car in line.

I remember Mom commenting with a chuckle that it looked like the DMV tester wasn't mad, so the person must have passed. Finally it was our turn and the tester walked up to our car. He asked for Mom's name and address, wrote them on the form attached to his clipboard and entered our car. He told mom to start the car, proceed up the street to the first red light, and turn left onto Main Street using the proper signals. I would like to report that we made it to Main Street, but I can't.

Mom started the car as directed, however, in her nervousness, popped the clutch with the engine racing, and flew out in to traffic without looking or signaling at all. There was a screeching of tires and horns blaring as she cut right in front of cars coming down the street. To make matters worse, when she heard the screeching tires and horns blowing, she panicked, floor boarded the gas pedal, causing the tester and me to fly back in our seats. She then slammed on the brakes, skidding into a car that had stopped at the red light.

The impact threw me into the back of the passenger seat, as the tester flew into the dash. Mom calmly said "I guess I failed?" After gaining his composure, the tester picked up the clip board he dropped while flying into the dash and stamped the form "FAILED," then bailed out of our car.

Undaunted, mom returned the next Monday for her second try at the test. As the tester approached our car, I could see trepidation in his face, however, he professionally filled out the test form and entered our car. Mom informed him that she had practiced pulling out into traffic, looking for other cars, and using the proper signals, so this time it would be a "snap."

It was a snap, until after looking for other cars, using her hand signals, and the car's left turn signal, she pulled on to the street. She was so happy that she accomplished the first stage of the test; she looked over at the tester and with a big smile said "How did I do?"

At that at that moment the light at the corner turned red. As Mom looked back at the street she saw that the car in front of us had stopped. Mom realized she could not stop quickly enough to keep from hitting the stopped car, and yanked the steering wheel to the right causing our car to veer over the curb and on to the side walk. The impact with the curb threw the tester up against his door and then jolted him back over to the driver's side of the car where he landed in mom's lap. This time he lost his composure and swore under his breath

"D_ _ _ crazy lady," stamped "FAILED" on the form as he jumped out of our car running back towards the test area. As I crawled into the front seat Mom observed, "He seems to get upset easily."

Sure enough, there we were the next Monday, in line for the third try. I could see the tester nervously looking back at us with a scowl on his face each time he got into the cars ahead of us. When it was our turn, the tester walked up to mom's window in the car, ripped off the test form, stamped it "PASSED," handed it through her window and just walked away! Mom laughed, commenting, "See Bobby, the third time was a charm" as she drove away, a fully licensed driver.

In June of 1954 Dad bought another beautiful new Buick Century. The second week after he purchased it, he made the mistake of parking it behind Mom's Pontiac. Dad and I were working on a culvert at the end of our driveway when Mom came out of the house to get in her car to go where she always did, "To the store."

When Mom saw that her car was blocked in, she asked dad if she could drive his car. Dad reluctantly agreed with the warning to "Take it easy on my new baby." About an hour later, as we were finishing the work on the driveway we heard a high pitched whistling noise along with a car engine knocking and sputtering. To Dad's horror, there came Mom driving his "new baby" with it whistling, knocking, and steam pouring out from under the hood. As she pulled into our driveway we could see that the entire grill of the car was full of wheat. Mom explained that as she was looking over at a beautiful new home on Newstead Road, she accidentally drove off into a field full of wheat. She said that it took a while to find her way out of the field because the wheat was so high.

After Dad and I cleaned the wheat Mom had combined out of the grill and radiator, we drove to Newstead Road to see Mom's wheat field. The field was located right by a bridge over another road. Even dad, as furious as he was, had to laugh as we drove up on the bridge and got a good view the maze Mom had created as she drove around in circles and "S" shapes trying to find her way out.

During her driving career she brought at least a dozen "YIELD" and "STOP" signs home stuck to various parts in and under her cars. One evening I received a call from a local gas station owner, asking me to have "Gerty" bring back the hose and nozzle she ripped off from the gas pump when she left his station.

Her escapades with the police were also legendary. One afternoon as mom and I were leaving the Village of Akron after one of her shopping sprees, a New York State Trooper tried to get Mom to pull over because she was speeding. As the Trooper drove close behind us with his red emergency light flashing and siren blaring, Mom totally ignored him and kept right on driving. We drove about three miles with the police car in hot pursuit.

When we got on the main road outside of the village, Mom declared, "If that cop doesn't pass me, I will have to step on it and create a little distance between us," which she accomplished by floor boarding the gas pedal, causing our car to accelerate to over 70 miles-per-hour. As we got near our house Mom decided that she had to get a gallon of milk from Kutters Cheese Factory located on the opposite side of the road from the direction which we were traveling. She drove right across the west bound lane and pulled into the store's parking lot with out signaling and slid up to the front of the building in a cloud of dust with the police car sliding right up behind us.

The Trooper flew out of his car scrambling over to our car, mad as a hornet. Mom calmly rolled down her window as he approached. He screamed that he had been chasing her for over four miles and inquired as to why she didn't stop when she heard the siren and saw his emergency lights flashing? He also emphatically asked if she knew the speed limit in the Village of Akron.

Mom, very deliberately opened her purse retrieving a pad and pencil from it. The Trooper asked what she was doing only to have Mom pertly reply that she was copying down his name, badge number, and that she also wanted the name of his supervising officer, because, if he didn't know the speed limit in Akron he shouldn't be a cop! At that moment I thought we were in grave peril, and Mom was surely going to jail. The Trooper just stood there seething, dumfounded for a moment, then said "GO TO H_ _ _ Lady," walked back to his police car and sped off.

One rainy morning, I received a call from Mom telling me that she was in "big trouble" in the City of Batavia Court. It seems that when Mom was going to turn into the parking lot of the Sylvania Television Plant where she worked, she didn't see the police officer directing traffic even though he had a bright florescent orange rain coat on.

To complicate her defense, the police officer testified that he was standing next to his patrol car which had its red emergency lights flashing, and that he was also holding bright flash lights in each of his hands. Additionally, he testified that just as Mom was about to run him over, he jumped up in the air, landing on the hood of her car, hanging to the windshield wipers for dear life as she kept right on driving into the parking lot.

Having a man suddenly on her hood, glaring in through the windshield at her, was more than Mom could handle. She slammed on the brakes catapulting the police officer off her hood and across the parking lot. Thank God he wasn't seriously hurt, only suffering bumps, bruises, and a few superficial cuts. Mom cried and carried on so much that the police officer even asked the judge to be lenient.

There are volumes of hilarious stories about Mom's exploits behind the wheel of an automobile; literally everyone who knew her has some story of their wild experiences riding with her. Everyone who knew of her driving escapades laughs when I share that at the age of 84, when Mom stopped driving, everyone in the United States received a $100 rebate on their car insurance.

Mom, who everyone referred to as "Grandma Gert," was a loving person with a wonderful personality. She was always singing and teaching Christian songs to the myriad of young people she constantly taxied to stores, restaurants, or anywhere else she or they desired to go. She could spend money faster than anyone in existence. Dad loved to harass Mom by repeating what Grandpa John told him the first time they met, "Gert will throw it out the back door, faster than you'll be able to bring it in the front door," referring to money, and Mom's spending habits.

Mom just lived in her own little world and that world revolved around spoiling me, shopping, dining out, and having fun doing them all. Those habits were a constant cause of friction between Dad and her. Dad had been brought up in Oklahoma, the son of a farmer, Arthur Alexander, whose wife, Stella, was a Native American from an Oklahoma Indian Reservation. Extremely poor, they lost what little they had, including their farm during the "dust bowl drought" of the late 1920s.

They moved to Illinois, where Dad's father's family had already migrated. With in a few years of living there, Dads father told Stella that he was moving to New York in hopes of starting a new life in the booming industrial economy near Buffalo. He asked her if she wanted to join him, however, she decided to stay in Illinois. Dad was given the option to stay in Illinois with his Mother or leave with his Father; he chose to go with his Dad.

Dad's family had been so poor he often had to eat bread covered with a layer of used cooking grease for both lunch and dinner. He only attended grammar school and by the time he was 12 years old, was already working to help support the family. When he arrived in New York, dad got a job in the Gypsum mines. He joined the Navy during World War II, serving from 1941 through 1945. After the war he was hired at the Chevrolet Plant in Buffalo. Because of his background and struggle to survive, he found Mom's cavalier attitude about money detestable.

Mom didn't help matters, as she broke every rule dad set down for conservation of energy and resources. She would turn the thermostat on the furnace up to 85 degrees if she was cold, and then open windows because it was so hot. She left lights on in every room in the house and the outside flood lights on, day and night. Dad would get so furious he would grab Mom by her neck and threaten to strangle her to death if he found the heat above seventy and lights on all over the house. He also reverted to taking the fuses for the lights and furnace with him to work, resulting in a very cold and dark house while he was gone.

Sometimes I would seek sanctuary at either Bruce or Dale's house. Other times I would find a blown out fuse and put a penny behind it causing the power to work for the furnace. I would hover over a heat register wrapped in a blanket in the dark until I would get warm, removing the penny before Dad came home. At times I would be so depressed that the walls in the rooms seemed to be gigantic and closing in on me. I came to feel that I would never escape pain and heartache and that I was worthless.

In an attempt to find an environment that was safe, secure, and rewarding I joined the Boy Scouts of America. I immersed my self in the community projects, paper drives, and camping trips. Because of my personality and hard work I found favor with the Scout leaders. I was the youngest scout in our Troop to be chosen for Junior Leader Training and the prestigious, Order of the Arrow. Little did I know that my illusion of safety would be shattered when in my third year at our week of summer camp, an Assistant Scout Master attempted to sodomize me.

That was the end of Boy Scouts. I again was plunged into deep despair and struggled to bury my inner rage and fears. After the Boy Scout trauma I remember thinking that life really sucks and there was no place to run and no place to hide.

CHAPTER 6

BECOMING SO MANY PEOPLE

—ꝏ—

In spite of the continuing battle between Mom and Dad, occasionally the family environment seemed almost normal and we experienced some good times. Most of them occurred when we would go on vacation to Illinois or Colorado to visit Dad's relatives. Dad's mother, Stella, still lived in Decatur, Illinois along with many of his aunts, uncles, and cousins. Dad's Uncle, Orie Alexander, raised Arabian show horses which I loved to watch being trained. I also enjoyed going to Dad's cousin Midge's home were I would play baseball with her children. However, for me the highlight in Illinois was riding the giant combines my cousins used to harvest the vast wheat fields on their farms.

When we went to Grandma Stella's house it was like going to another world. She provided housing for numerous alcoholics who lived with her for years. Treating them like they were her own children, she always made excuses for them being drunk. The environment could only be described as a disaster area with any number of "her boys," sleeping on ratty old couches, filthy over stuffed chairs, or the floor.

The floor was so dirty it looked like it had never been swept or mopped. The dining room table was completely covered with moldy pots, pans, dirty plates, and silverware.

Cockroaches scurried everywhere and the stench was almost unbearable. I wondered what Dad must have experienced as a young boy living with her. I certainly understood why he chose to move to New York with his Father.

Grandma Stella was one hundred percent American Indian and practiced what she called a Native Indian Religion, which bordered on Voodoo. She would chant incantations with her eyes tightly closed. Then suddenly her eyes would pop wide open and roll back into her head. She would scream, seeing visions of people who she said were dead but were communicating with her, and predicting future events. Her trances scared me half to death and I was always glad when she came out of them.

Our trips to Trinidad, Colorado to visit Dad's sister Frieda were filled with stops to see the wonders of the Rocky Mountains. One of those wonders we always visited was the Royal Gorge which had the highest suspension bridge in the world. The bridge spanned the vast gap from one mountain peak to another high above the Colorado River. At times the wind caused the bridge to tilt to an angle which made it impossible to drive across.

The gorge also had a cable car descending almost straight down the mountain to the river below. It was exciting to drive across the swaying bridge but almost indescribable to ride the cable car down the face of the mountain. I bravely proclaimed that I wanted to ride in the front seat, then in sheer terror closed my eyes for most of the trip.

The town of Trinidad, where Aunt Frieda lived, was nestled below twin mountain peeks. One peek housed a large sign with the name Trinidad on it, and the other peek housed Aunt Freda and her husband Hal's house. Their house was extremely large and resembling an ancient castle on a mountain top. There were 26 rooms with two towers on the front corners of the house. One of the towers housed a bedroom that I slept in. I felt like the King of Trinidad, picturing myself as a Knight in King Arthur's Court.

Aunt Freda and Uncle Hal hosted our trips to Taos, New Mexico to visit the Pueblo Indian Reservation. The Reservation was a tourist attraction because of its adobe houses made of clay and straw, with thick walls and roofs. The Indian people charged a dollar to have our picture taken with them. They also sold jewelry made of turquoise, which Dad loved to barter for.

After visiting the Pueblo Reservation we would travel to Cimarron, New Mexico to attend a rodeo. The main dish at the rodeo was barbequed burgers made from Buffalo meat. No trip to New Mexico was complete until we ate at an authentic Mexican Restaurant featuring the hottest Mexican chili imaginable. Dad challenged me to eat a bowl of hot green chili, promising that if I could eat the entire contents of the bowl, he would buy me a go-cart. As hard as I tried, I never finished half of a bowl. What I did accomplish, however, was to burn my mouth and tongue beyond measure, and won't even attempt to describe the next day at the other end.

It was good to have a respite from the constant antagonism between Mom and Dad, those vacations were like Heaven. Unfortunately Heaven only lasted two weeks and heartache always followed. I experienced terrible bouts of depression after the vacations as I anticipated another world war starting between them.

I gauged how things were going by the songs Dad listened to on our record player. If he listened to the song, "Oh My Papa," things were pretty cool; however, if war was heating up, he would listen to a song by Frankie Lane named "Jezebel," playing it over and over with the volume extremely high. The wonderful home life I once experienced full of security, love, and Jesus, had faded into a distant memory.

In school I was very popular having many friends, and I excelled at sports, especially baseball and basketball. The teachers always experienced a dilemma when it came time to pass or fail me based on my academic performance. I seldom did homework and my parents never attended parent/teacher conferences or responded to the letters sent home showing that my academic performance was unsatisfactory.

However, when the State Achievement Tests, which gauged comprehension, were given at the end of each year, I scored extremely high on them. I remember overhearing one of my teachers asking the principal how they could justify failing me, when I scored the highest marks on the State Achievement Tests. The end result was that I never repeated a grade and only failed one course my entire 12 years in school.

I remember the teacher who failed me in Junior English. She told me that I had such tremendous potential and because she cared for me, wouldn't let me off the hook just because I could absorb enough in class to pass every test. I wish I could find her today so I could hug her and thank her for caring enough to fail me.

I was continually at battle with myself. I knew and wanted to conform to what was socially and academically acceptable, which would have resulted in positive rewards. However, the lack of parental involvement or control in my life left me to my own devices. I knew I should have gone to school on Monday; however, it was more fun to go fishing or hunting.

To survive I developed three personalities, one very affable, attempting to meet social and academic norms and values. The second personality was defiant, always pushing the envelope, and was the product of immaturity and the lack of adult guidance. It resulted in the inability to reach acceptable norms and values.

The third personality gave me the ability to survive by establishing an environment where I was in total control. This survival personality rejected all social and academic norms, values, and authority figures. I became willing to accept any consequences regardless of their severity to do whatever met my needs. It was extremely rewarding to skip school on Mondays to go fishing or hunting even if the truant officer was always in hot pursuit. I didn't care that I had to stay after school for detention on Tuesdays, because I controlled my life and environment on Mondays, and therefore, Mondays didn't hurt.

Just as I was getting used to a life where Mom and Dad were so busy working and battling each other, that they didn't have time to control or parent me, Ed got discharged from the Army. I was ecstatic, my savior had come back home to me, my identity was back; I was Ed Alexander's little brother and he was going to protect and take care of me again.

The first thing he instituted was me going to school everyday. I didn't mind Monday school because when I came home I could drive Ed's car around the lot next to our house until he came home from work. Ed was employed at a construction company and rode to work with his fellow employees.

Ed let me drive his car around as long as I didn't go on the road and washed it before he came home. After a few months on the job he bought a new 1959 Ford Galaxy 500XL convertible. As soon as I returned home from school, I would jump in that beauty, put the top down, and continuously drive up and down the driveway and around our house. Every now and then I'd go for a little jaunt up and down our road. Of course, Bruce Fisher's mother, Ruthie couldn't wait to rat me out for driving on the road. Ed knew I was testing my driving skills out on the road and warned me, "Bobby, just be careful and don't hit any thing."

To me, my brother was the coolest person alive, however, there was something different about Ed; he had learned to drink excessively while in the Army. Because he stopped for a "few beers," every night on the way home from work, I always had time to drive around a while before cleaning his car. Every Friday, I washed and waxed that beautiful Ford convertible so Ed could cruise around in style.

His weekends consisted of going out to the local clubs and bars with his drinking buddies, looking to pick up girls. He usually came home very late, and very drunk. Naturally, he wanted to sleep in on Saturday mornings because of his hangover, however, he always dragged himself out of bed to drive me to intramural roller skating and basketball programs.

In appreciation for him taking me to intramurals I would again, clean and prepare the car for his Saturday night escapades. I also enjoyed cleaning his car because there would be a full can of beer or two left over from Friday night. When I finished cleaning, I would drive behind our house while drinking a left over beer, dreaming of going to the bars with Ed. There was only one thing I knew for sure, I wanted to be just like my brother Ed.

It wasn't very long before the worst thing I could imagine happened. I started to lose him again, this time to a woman, his new girl friend, Claudia Whitman. After six months of dating they were married. I remember the wedding ceremony, but that was about all because by the time Dad realized that I was drinking the spiked punch, I was already bombed. Mom and Dad actually thought it was a little funny because there I was 15 years old, standing right in the middle of Ed's close friends, drink in hand, carrying on as if I was just one of the guys. For me it was a rite of passage, showing that while I knew I was losing Ed, I was going to follow in his footsteps.

After Ed's marriage, home life went back to being the same old dysfunctional environment. At times Mom and Dad seemed to be getting along, but most of the time they were at war. As their relationship became more and more strained and hostile, life became extremely depressing. There I was right in the middle of their battles again. It was almost like they wanted me to choose sides but I couldn't, I loved them both so very much.

Dad had accepted and treated me like I was his own flesh and blood since I was six years old and let me assume his last name. I was the center of Mom's life and she spoiled me rotten, letting me do any thing I wanted to with little or no control. While I enjoyed being able to manipulate Mom, I also liked the stability of Dad's guidance. It was maddening to be around them though. We would be sitting at the dinner table; Dad would ask me, "How was school today son?" and I would say "Good." Almost immediately Mom would ask me the exact same question, "How was school today?" I responded, "Good." Some times I would cross them up by telling one that it went terrible and the other it went good. What was extremely frustrating and drove me absolutely insane was that neither one of them would acknowledge that I had just told the other one the exact opposite answer moments before. The same crazy drill occurred when one would ask if I had any home work.

The only time I experienced them acting as though we were still a normal family was when Mrs. Hanley, the high school truant officer, unexpectedly came to our house one night as we were eating dinner. She came to address the fact that I was again skipping school every Monday. Dad put his arm around Mom as they walked Mrs. Hanley to the door, promising that they would punish me and see that I never missed a Monday again. Ha ha ha, they went right back to separately telling me that each of them was embarrassed, each separately exhorting me to attend school on Mondays. I did go to school the next Monday, but was back to skipping with in two weeks. The funny thing was, Mrs. Hanley never came back, and they believed that I was going on Mondays!

CHAPTER 7

HERE COMES THE NIGHT

—∿∿—

As conditions at home escalated to all out war, I realized the end was near, another of my families had crashed and burned; there was going to be a divorce. After being in the middle for so long it was almost a relief when Mom and Dad stopped interacting in any way. As I reflected on my life I came to the conclusion there must be something dreadfully wrong with me. My real Father had abandoned me, my real Mother gave me away, my first Step-father, a Christian, abandoned me, and now my third Father was about to discard me.

A deep seated depression like a dark cloud totally engulfed my very existence. I was "no good," a throw away child, not worthy of love. I couldn't look into a mirror, if I did, I would see an extremely grotesque reflection. I heard voices telling me I was worthless and no one could love me. At times the walls seemed like they were closing in on me and the furniture looked gigantic. I swore an oath to myself that I would never treat anyone the way I was treated, if I ever had children, they would be loved, protected, and never abandoned. At that instant the Devil laughed and said, "Oh yeah, just watch! Just watch!"

I was consumed with anger; a river of rage roared just below the surface of my easy going care free veneer. However, I didn't have the strength or ability to deal with or vent these terrible hidden feelings. The only escape I could find was in the artificial environment created by consuming alcohol so I conned my naïve Mother into buying beer for me. Here I was, 16 years old and my Mom was buying me beer.

I also drank the wine and whiskey stored in our liquor cabinet. Because, neither Mom nor Dad drank alcohol with any regularity, they seldom if ever checked the liquor cabinet. Besides, now that the family was breaking up, the liquor and wine brought out for holidays and other family events was the farthest thing from their minds. I enjoyed drinking wine, but had to dilute the whiskey to make it palatable. Consuming alcohol resulted in euphoric feelings that numbed my pain and helped me escape from reality. Locking myself in my bedroom drinking wine allowed me to insulate myself from the anguish and rage that tormented my soul.

I kept up a good facade at school enjoying my popularity and leadership role as class treasurer, while burying myself in sports. However, the teachers and administrators used a blatant double standard within the academic and social norms of the high school which ignited a rebellion within me. When you came from "a bad family environment," it was easy for administrators, teachers, and almost everyone else in a supervisory position to stereotype you with what I call the scarlet letter, "L," which meant "Loser."

Once you were branded a loser, everything you did was evaluated through a skewed standard. If a loser writes a paper, it will receive a low and/or failing grade no matter how good the contents may be. For example, I convinced one of the golden students to switch English papers with me. You know the golden ones; they have the good family names in the community, their parents have attended every parent /

teacher conference and sporting event, helped out in the class room, and chaperoned every field trip since Kindergarten. I turned in her paper with my name on it and she turned in mine.

The results; she received an A, and I received a C -. She had never received a grade lower than B + on any paper or home work assignment in her life. When I challenged the teacher, asking why I received the C- grade on my paper, she indigently told me that the content was "weak, as usual!" I then dropped the bomb, declaring that I had switched papers with an "A" student, who of course received an A on my paper while I received C- on hers.

I was expelled for a week, while my co-conspirator received a scolding from the teacher and administration for helping me with "my deception." Knowing that my family wouldn't come to my defense allowed the administration to severely discipline me. They hid behind the "setting an example that deception is a terrible façade to divert their hypocrisy and mask their double standards which were the real issues. I didn't mind the week external suspension, in fact, enjoyed it. However, I was now branded as "a loser" and an "incorrigible disciplinary problem," it was open season on me.

What the administrators and teachers didn't realize was that their actions motivated me to declare war on the school. This war provided an avenue for venting some of the growing hate and rage within me. I now openly rebelled, attacking every structural, social, academic, and administrative value they held so dear. I remember the guidance counselor fueling the war by telling one of my best friends Charlie Klotzbach and I, that we should consider being truck drivers or farmers, because we were, "Too stupid to do any thing else."

While I had respect for truck drivers and farmers, my vision, was of being a doctor, lawyer, or some other type of professional. Incidentally, Charlie, the should be truck driver, actually became the superintendent of a large oil distribution company. What really drove the teachers and administrators crazy was that I could absorb enough in the classroom, and complete just enough academic work to keep from failing. I remember a teacher commenting to the school superintendent Mr. Lane, who hated me with a passion; that my high IQ resulted in my "beating the system." One area where the superintendent thought he could torment me was in my love of playing sports.

I had been a star basketball player on the high school team. Mr. Lane told the coach he could only let me play during the last minute of each basketball game. He thought that by hurting me in the one area where I excelled and loved, he would win the war. The basketball coach resigned over Mr. Lane's ultimatum; however I told him I respected his decision to resign rather than carry out the superintendent's "Vendetta," but if he resigned, Mr. Lane would have won. Coach withdrew his resignation, and I played one minute of each game, staring right in the superintendent's eyes as each game ended. I refused to show one speck of the pain raging inside of me, a rage that fueled my resolve to win the war.

Using his position as superintendent, Mr. Lane also tried to remove me as class treasurer by instituting a rule whereby all class officers had to carry at least a B average. My classmates rejected his attempt to remove me by declaring that our class had duly elected me treasurer all four high school years and it was their prerogative to elect whosoever they desired with out interference from the administration. He backed down and I remained treasurer. The only thing I regret was that after our class graduation ceremony I told Mr. Lane that when he died I was going to urinate and defecate on his grave. I had lowered myself to his standards, however, I wanted him to know that at some point I would exact my revenge and he wouldn't be able to do a thing about it. Yes, revenge is a meal best served cold!

One thing is very true, leave a teenager to his own devices and he will find trouble. With our family in shambles, I searched for something to take its place and found it in the family of a classmate, George Rooney. George was a transfer student from a neighboring school district with an extremely interesting family, to say the least.

His father, George Sr., who everyone called "the Old Man," was an alcoholic, as was his mother, Irene, who everyone called "the Old Lady." The Old Man was an iron worker in the construction industry. He seldom worked more than the 20 weeks, which then qualified him for unemployment payments for six months. The result was that the Rooney's seldom had enough money to live above the poverty level.

Any money the Old Man made when he did work was almost always spent long before he returned home. When he received his paycheck, he often headed to Buffalo on a "toot." A toot was when a person would go to bars, continuously drinking until every penny he had was spent. This could take days or even a week, because usually there would be three or four other iron workers with their paychecks, joining the binge drinking.

There were always bars intentionally situated in close proximity to the Iron Worker Union Headquarters just to accommodate the workers. At times we would try to bring the Old Man home from the bar before he was completely broke, however, most of the time that was a lost cause so we waited for the inevitable call from a bar or police department, to pick him up. Things were better when he was on unemployment because his unemployment checks were mailed directly to their house. This allowed the Old Lady to go to the bank and take enough money out of it to buy a few groceries, cigarettes, and the case (24 bottles) of Iroquois beer they consumed every day.

Life in the Rooney home totally revolved around drinking beer and smoking cigarettes. Their house was always dirty, windows so coated with nicotine that they were hard to see through, floors seldom swept or mopped. The walls had no paint, and there were holes punched through them allowing you to see into almost every room with out opening the doors. Beds consisted of open metal coil springs, covered by stained mattresses with no sheets. Almost everything they owned came from the Salvation Army Thrift Store, rummage sales, or donations. They procured food from the U.S. Government surplus distribution centers, usually oatmeal, cheese, and spam. We ate a lot of spam and cheese sandwiches chased down with a bottle of beer.

Every night as the Old Man and Old Lady became drunk they would swear at each other profusely, usually escalating their battle to the practice of throwing the empty beer bottles at each other. The good thing was that the Old Lady sat in an overstuffed chair in the living room, while the Old Man sat at the dining room table making them about 30 feet apart. The result of this distance was that most of the beer bottle missiles missed their targets.

It was hilarious for George Jr., his younger brother Billy, nicknamed Willie Gump, and I to moderate the verbal and beer bottle wars. We pretended we were radio announcers describing the Friday Night Fights. "Ladies and Gentlemen the Friday Night Fights are on the air. In the living room, weighing in at 120 pounds, the undefeated champion of beer bottle throwing, the Irish Old Lady, Irene Rooney! The challenger, in the dining room, weighing in at 160 pounds, Irish Old Man Rooney!"

Besides being ring announcers, we also were beer fetchers, charging one bottle of beer for us to share, for each bottle we delivered. The Iroquois beer, (actually Iroquois Ale), they drank had the rottenest taste; we described as "bilge water." However, rotten tasting Iroquois Ale was better than no Ale at all. Quite often I would procure money from Mom, pay for the Old Man's case of Iroquois Ale in return for him purchasing a case of our favorite, Genesee Beer.

The majority of time we did our drinking at the Rooney's house, however, at times we went to local bars with the Old Man. I usually provided money, which he referred to as "scratch," to finance the escapade. In the 1960's the legal age to drink alcoholic beverage in New York State was 18 years old. Because every male 18 years of age had to register for the draft, bars required your draft card for proof of age. It was easy to manufacture fake draft cards, so almost everyone underage had one. The name, Edward Edsel appeared on my counterfeit draft card for two reasons, first, the Edsel automobile was popular, and second, I didn't want anyone to know my real name, especially the police.

When you made rounds of the local bars with the Rooney's and their extended family, Aunt Witch Rooney, whose real first name was Rita, her husband Uncle Daisy Rooney, whose real first name was Dave, and cousin John, who everyone called "the Leech," you could guarantee there was going to be a bar fight. The fights sometimes resulted in the police being called, so you never wanted to be in possession of a document which authentically identified you. The Old Man, George Rooney Senior, was the brother of Uncle Daisy (Dave) Rooney, Aunt Witch (Rita) Rooney; Dave's wife was the sister of the Old Lady, Irene Rooney. I don't think anyone outside the Rooney family knew Aunt Witch's real first name; everyone just called her "the Witch." I once sent a postcard from Daytona Beach Florida addressed: The Witch, Darien, New York, sure enough, she received it without delay.

Everything in the Rooney's life was geared to obtaining money so they wouldn't run out of beer. If we were drinking at their house, we played the card game Euchre for beer, and at the bars we played it for money, cheating to win. The problem in bars was that everyone cheated, so winning came down to who could out-cheat whom. Most bars had shuffle board, bowling machines, pinball machines, and pool tables, all used for gambling.

We would set people up called "fish," taking their money by getting an unsuspecting person to join in a foursome pinball, bowling, or pool game, as a partner of one of the other three players. What the fish didn't know was that the other three players were part of our crew. Each player would put $10 in the kitty, the winning team taking all. Unfortunately whatever team the fish was on, some how always lost. We often changed partners so the fish never caught on. Within a few games the fish left and we split the winnings repeating the process when a new fish arrived. If the atmosphere in the bars was slow or boring, someone would start a bar fight to liven things up a little. Because we always would be right in the middle of most of them, I developed very good fighting skills.

The more I became aware of the barroom code of silence, the more I realized they were perfect venues to vent the raging storm boiling inside me. If the police responded to a fight in a bar no one knew anything. I would drink beer until my conscience was overpowered, always ready to fight at the least provocation, fighting any and everyone who even looked cross eyed at me.

I loved to fight middle aged men because you gained stature with the barroom regulars if you beat up someone bigger or older than you. I used these fights to vicariously batter the people who caused so much pain in my life. I was a five foot ten inch, 150 pound, skinny, 17 year old kid, beating up 200 pound 25 year olds. When rage is your motivation, it is amazing the strength you possess.

Just when George Jr. and I were making our mark in the barroom fight scene, we received an added bonus by befriending another teenager named Bill Daube. Bill, whose family called him Willie, was one of ten brothers whose father, Bruno, moved to Corfu, New York, to help his brother, Hans, manage the family meat packing plant. Willie and his brothers were tough as nails and loved to fight; practicing on each other when there was no one else available to mix it up with.

Willie had boxed in the golden gloves tournaments in western Ohio, before moving to Corfu and we gladly welcomed him into our click. From the moment he joined up with us, two things happened, first, we never lost a fight in a bar again, and second, we had girls swarming all over us. Not only was Willie a great boxer, he was also extremely handsome, or as the girls crooned, "Drop-dead-gorgeous." In every bar we frequented, girls would hang all over him, which meant there were plenty of the second stringers for George and me.

In school, George, Willie, and I were tagged as the "Three Musketeer Trouble Makers" resulting in the administration and teachers attempting to intimidate us, physically and mentally. In 1963 teachers and administrators routinely roughed and sometimes beat up students with no repercussions whatsoever. There was a teacher named Roland Carney, who was a wild man. At least once a day he would grab a student with his hands griped tightly around the poor slob's neck, slam him into the wall or lockers just to make a statement and keep everyone in line. Our gym teacher was a former lineman on his college football team. Teachers would inform him of students who needed an attitude adjustment and he delighted in dispensing "motivational butt kicking's." I can attest to his ability to do just that.

George, Willie, and I usually skipped school on Mondays, spending the day bowling and playing cards. The truant officer knew we were hanging out, at Andrews Bowling Alley and barroom, however, never pursued us there. Maybe she was intimidated, as many school officials were, after

Willie knocked out a teacher who tried to physically intimidate him. Willie was suspended for two weeks; however, after the incident teachers and administrators all backed off and stopped harassing us.

As class treasurer, I was very resourceful at developing avenues to raise funds. We had bake and rummage sales, however, I hit the jack pot when I designed sweatshirts featuring our school name, Corfu High School, and our logo, a giant green dragon. Sales were phenomenal, every one, students, teachers, administrators, and parents, all purchased them. Because of my hard work designing, producing, marketing, and selling the sweatshirts, I considered it only fair that our class finance a vacation, for George, Willie, and me to attend spring break at Daytona Beach, Florida. I raided the sweatshirt fund, taking $150 and purchased a 1954 Ford station wagon for $100. With the $100 Mom donated toward the trip, we had $150 for our expenses. The plan was to sell the car, which was worth at least $150, when we returned from Florida, so I could replace what I borrowed from the sweat shirt fund before our class advisor realized it was missing.

We had a terrific time at Daytona Beach and things were going just as I planned until, on our way back to New York, the car's transmission burnt out. Luckily we were only ten miles from home and less than a mile from Stanley Staba's junk yard. Stanley towed the car to his junk yard but unfortunately, after his towing charge, only paid us $30 for it. That left us $120 short when replacing the sweatshirt money. I am not sure why our class advisor never noticed $150 missing from the sweatshirt fund. Maybe it was because he was the shop teacher or maybe he was also skimming from the fund. For whatever reason, it was never missed or accounted for. At our ten-year class reunion, George and I thanked everyone for sponsoring our 1963 spring break trip to Daytona Beach, and offered to pay back the $150. It was the highlight of the night's stories.

As our senior year was closing in on graduation, I wasn't sure if I would be allowed to graduate due to my comments on the State Education Department's mandatory Regents Examinations. I decided my final act of rebellion against the favoritism and general hypocrisy with in the school system, would be refusing to take the Regents exams. After all they were only given to see if a student would get an honored "Regents Diploma" versus a General Diploma.

I acquiesced and decided to take the tests because I was told to take them or automatically be disqualified from graduating. Upon completion of the tests everyone was required to write, I do so declare and sign their name after the final question. As a final reminder of my rebellion, I wrote the following on the bottom of all my final Regents Tests: "Kiss my A_ _, I do so declare!" signed Robert E. Alexander.

George and I graduated on June 23, 1963. I ranked sixty-two and George, sixty-three, in a graduating class of sixty-three students.

No one from either family attended the ceremony.

CHAPTER 8

THE WILD BLUE YONDER

—⟶⟨⟨⟨⟶—

With in three months after graduation George and Willie enlisted in the United States Air Force, trying to convince me to sign up with them. I was tempted to join, however, I wasn't ready to commit to four years in anything. With my two best friends and drinking buddies gone, I wandered around aimlessly, drinking, fighting, and working menial jobs.

When George and Willie came home on leave, I realized I should have enlisted with them. Just seeing my two buddies all spruced up in their dress blue United States Air Force uniforms fostered enough jealousy to compel me to join up. George was assigned to work in altitude chambers, training pilots on the effects of barometric pressure change in flight. Willie was assigned to an air refueling squadron in Germany. On May 1, 1964, there I was enlisting in the Air Force.

After I signed my enlistment commitment papers and was sworn in, my recruiter dropped an atomic bomb on me. Because Dad Alexander hadn't formally adopted me, I was *not* legally Robert Alexander, I was Robert Faulring, and must serve under my legal name. I vehemently protested, telling the recruiter, I would refuse to leave for basic training if I couldn't serve as Robert Alexander, arguing that my school records were in the Alexander name. However, the recruiter gave me two options; I would either go to basic training as Airman Robert Faulring or Leavenworth Military Prison as Robert Alexander. I asked when I was leaving for Lackland Air Force Training Center.

While I acquiesced, I was totally devastated by having to use a name I hated and hadn't used since I was six years old. I felt as if my identity was being stolen. Using John Faulring's last name again, brought flashbacks of the day he abandoned me. My mind vividly replayed Grandpa holding me up so I could look out of our basement window watching Daddy John slowly back out of the driveway. I experienced extreme anguish as I realized I would have to live as Robert Faulring the next four years. Just imagine for a moment, after 12 years of using a different last name, you had to reassume the name of a father who abandoned you, left the state to avoid paying child support to help you, and did not care if you lived or died. How would you feel about using his last name again?

There were repercussions of having to use Faulring as my last name. The first was actually funny. When I, along with other recruits, arrived at Lackland Air force Base in San Antonio, Texas for basic military training, we were ordered to form two lines, and yell out "Here sir," when our names were called. Our drill instructor, hereafter referred to as D.I. called out our each name; the recruit answered "Here Sir," and D.I. then assigned a squad.

"Adams!"

"Here Sir."

"Squad A."

"Bradington!"

"Here Sir."

"Squad B."

Everything went just fine, until "Faulring, (no answer), "Faulring?"(still silence) FA U L R I N G, are you here boy?" At that instant I realized he was calling my name and yelled "Here Sir." There was a pause, "Don't you know your own name boy?" "No sir I don't." Our D.I. lost it. Replying that God must be punishing him for cheating on his wife and sending him the stupidest bunch of A_ _holes that ever arrived for basic training. He described us in glowing terms saying, "Half look like girls, the rest look like faggots, and one doesn't even know his F_ _ _ing name!"

The second repercussion was that the Batavia Daily News printed my Air Force picture with the name, Robert Faulring. Their narrative read, "Robert Faulring of Corfu, has joined the United States Air force and stationed at Lackland Air Force Base, Texas." Everyone who viewed the picture was convinced the newspaper printed someone else's name under my picture.

The eight-week basic training schedule was demanding: up at six a.m., wash, shave, and fly into our uniform to be in front of the barracks ready for inspection within ten-minutes. Anyone who was unable to complete those tasks in a timely fashion was rewarded with a mile run around the parade field.

Marching to the Mess Hall always brought new experiences for me. I was assigned to the right front Road Guard position. Front Road Guards marched approximately ten paces in front of our formation. When we approached a road crossing, D.I. would yell "Road Guards post," the signal for the two front Road Guards to blow their whistle and stop any and all traffic so our squad could pass through safely.

I experienced one problem as right front Road Guard; my ability to march to a cadence closely resembled Moms ability to drive a car. Our D.I. would call out cadence such as this, (one of his repeatable cadences): "G I beans and G I gravy, G I wish I joined the navy," the squad repeated, "G I

Beans and G I gravy, G I wish I joined the navy, Go to your left, your right, your left."

When we got to the, "Go to your left," I would almost always be on my right step prompting the D.I. to scream, "Your other left Faulring, or what ever your name is." I'd also find myself marching away thinking I was ten paces ahead of our squad, only to hear the D.I. scream sarcastically, "Faulring, we are over here, could you please come join us?" I would be nowhere near where I should have been.

When we arrived at the mess hall, we would stand at attention waiting for our turn to enter. There would be seven or eight squads of men standing at attention also waiting to go in and eat. The mess hall was divided into two separate sides, with squads of men recruits eating on one side, and squads of women recruits eating on the other side. We were never allowed to look at, much less talk to a female recruit.

One morning as we marched up to the front of the mess hall we ran head on into a female squad marching out of the mess hall area. Both D.I.'s called "halt" at the same time stopping each squad with their front Road Guards, nose to nose. I was standing at attention with my nose literally two inches from the female Road Guard's nose.

Our D.I. yelled, "Faulring, you better not look at her." I yelled back, "Sir, I have to look at her, we are at attention so I must have my eyes straight ahead and she is directly in front of me, sir." He replied, "You are right, good job Airman Faulring, so now you can tell her, you love her! Go ahead tell her you love her, but you better not smile!"

Have you ever tried not to smile when you are nose to nose with someone from the opposite sex, much less under those types of conditions? It was impossible, I burst out laughing, and so did she. At that instant the female D.I. screamed, "You don't have carnal desire for my recruit do you Airman Faulring?" Before I could respond she barked out the following, "Ladies, there is two-miles of male anatomy on this base and you aren't experiencing one little inch of it!" I couldn't resist, responding, "Ah, darn it." There I was running three-laps around the parade field after we returned to our barracks. I was also moved from front to rear Road Guard. Rear Road Guard was easy; just follow the rest of the squad.

Mail call was the highlight of any day. However, if you had squad duty such as Barracks Guard or cleaning of the latrines and showers, you were not allowed to read mail until the tasks were completed. I was on Barracks Guard duty one afternoon when mail call was held. Sure enough I received a letter from a girlfriend and was dying to read it.

In an attempt to read the letter with out being caught, I laid it in my helmet. As I was reading how she missed me and catching up on what was happening back home, a voice behind me softly asked if I was enjoying my letter? I replied yes about the same time I realized the voice was that of our D.I.! As punishment, he ordered me to stand Barracks Guard duty for 24-hours straight. At roll call the next morning he announced that recruit Faulring, "Gives me more trouble than my girlfriend downtown, she only calls my wife."

Thank God there was another recruit who messed up more than I did therefore diverting attention away from my transgressions. Abe as D.I. called him, was short, overweight, physically weak, and possessed what D.I. referred to as a "Classic Hymie," nose. Remember, back in 1964 there was no "political correctness" and D.I.'s often insulted everyone's nationality, race, and religion.

Abe's squeaky voice drove D.I. crazy. He would repeat everything, Abe said, in a mocking parakeet sounding tone. Abe didn't help matters, whining, "I want to go see the Rabbi," every time we were engaged in close order marching drills, calisthenics, or mile runs. On one of his trips to see the Rabbi, Abe sealed his fate, totally replacing me on the D.I.'s "Sh_ _ List."

We had just completed the marching drill as Abe waddled off toward the Rabbi's office. D.I. allowed a 20 minute break before and after the calisthenics because of the intense heat. The temperature was at least 85 degrees as the hot Texas sun beat down on us. The second break ended and we gulped a last swig of water in anticipation of the mile run. Lining up in double formation, we began the run. Just as we rounded the first turn on the parade grounds D.I. bellowed "Squad Halt."

Everyone nervously wondered who messed up causing the abrupt halt to our run, as we anticipated one of D.I.'s tirades and punishments. What we saw still brings a hearty laugh as I vividly replay the scene in my mind. "What in the blankety blank do we have here, Barbie?" D.I. barked. No one could believe their eyes. Here came Abe slowly walking up to our formation wearing a pair of pink heart-shaped baby sun glasses, *the kind you would see on a three year old little girl!*

There aren't enough adjectives in the entire dictionary to describe what he looked like. No one could hold their composure and everyone, including D.I., was roaring with laughter. Abe's response, "The sun is bright, you're just jealous because you didn't find them." When D.I. regained his composure, putting us back at attention, he informed Abe that he was not allowed to take the sun glasses off for the rest of basic training. D.I. meant exactly what he said, forcing Abe to sleep, shower, march, eat meals, and literally never take them off.

If a recruit continues to have problems adjusting to military training they can be set back to a previous level or discharged form the service. While I flirted with being set back, poor Abe was set back to a squad two weeks behind ours. In fact, when we finished basic training and were processing out of Lackland Air Force Base to transfer to our technical schools, there was Abe marching with a squad in its first week, clearly recognizable by those beautiful pink sun glasses. He gave us the thumbs up and quickly proclaimed that he was going to make it as he marched on by. I often wondered if he ever completed basic training and if he still had those sun glasses.

For me, it was off to Amarillo, Texas for training in my technical field, Fighter Jet Airplane mechanics. I was to learn how to repair fighter jets. The training was intense and challenging. We learned every component of fighter jets, including, fuselage, propulsion, hydraulics, ejection systems, fuel, and oxygen systems.

The good thing in tech school was that we were treated like professionals, training in a civilian airplane factory. There were a few basic military rules and regulations, marching to meals, dorm cleaning, etc…, however, the atmosphere was relaxed. On weekends we were free to leave the base dressed in civilian clothes. Many of us would head to Amarillo to explore the barrooms, clubs, and girls, all of which were there gladly waiting to take our money.

Almost everyone who went to Amarillo checked out the many tattoo shops, and even though I hated needles, at noon and stone sober, on July 4th 1964 a lady tattoo artist inked two tattoos on my arms. On the left arm an eagle with the United States Flag and USAF, while on the right and just as important, "Alex," my beloved nickname. All my buddies asked why I had Alex tattooed on my arm and I told them it was my "real name."

The tattoo shops were not very hygienic or sterile, covering new tattoos with paper napkins and scotch tape, which resulted in many tattoos becoming infected. Tattoo infections could result in disciplinary proceedings because we were damaging "Government Property." My tattoo never became infected, but some of the color on the flag was dug out while I was fighting in a bar that night.

Often, my closest buddies and I would rent Honda motorcycles on the weekends and cruise the hills of the North Texas panhandle. On other occasions we prowled the City of Amarillo hoping to hook up with the local talent. One Saturday night we decided to rent a room at the Amarillo Hotel and hire a prostitute. None of us had any experience in the fine art of contacting and hiring prostitutes, however, I figured bellhops and elevator operators were the key to any and all illegal activities in any hotel.

I informed the elevator attendant of what room we were in and our desire to find some female action. Sure enough with in ten minutes there was a pimp at our door, escorting a prostitute who claimed she was working her way through college by selling sexual favors. One close look at her revealed that she must have been attending college for quite some time.

Because the price for sex was $40 per person, we pooled $10 each, and flipped coins, the winner having sex with her. I lost, but wasn't upset, all I could think of was that she probably performed sex acts with hundreds of customers, and there was a high probability she may have a sexually transmitted disease.

When the pimp returned to pick up the prostitute, he asked if any of us played poker. I wish I would have been as cautious with the poker game as I was with the hooker. We were invited to the "big game" on the 6th floor. My buddy Johnny and I decided to pool $40 each, to take a stab at hitting the jackpot in the poker game. He would play the game while I "watched his back." One look at the five guys in the poker game was enough to justify why I needed to watch his back. They claimed to be traveling poker players going from city to city holding big Poker games.

I pulled Johnny aside expressing concern that we were being set up and couldn't win, just like the fish I hustled in the bars back home. Johnny assured me he knew exactly what he was doing. He predicted he would double or triple our money in short order. As skeptical as I was, I agreed to let him play, but warned him that I smelled "a rat."

Within nine or ten hands Johnny had doubled our money. I gave him the high sign to leave the game, sure by then, he was being set up. Johnny ignored my gestures, and with a quick wink, looked at his next hand. The poker game was Five Card Draw; Johnny was dealt a pair of queens. Discarding three cards, he was then dealt another queen along with a nine and ten. The dealer who had opened with a $5 bet, now bet $10, Johnny immediately raised that bet by another $10.

I could see the hand writing on the wall, the dealer then raised Johnny's bet by $20. Johnny raised back, another $20 with the dealer instantly raising the bet to $100. We didn't have a $100 but that didn't bother Johnny, he immediately called the $100 raise, flopping down his three queens declaring, "Read them, and weep boys." Read them and weep means you think you have the winning hand and the other player would be crying after losing. As you can imagine, the dealer miraculously had three kings, beating Johnny's hand. He immediately demanded the $100 Johnny didn't have.

As Johnny tried to assure the now irate dealer, that we would pay them when we received our paychecks at the end of the month, I saw the dealer reach for a pistol in his jacket. I grabbed Johnny by his arm yelled, "Gun," and dove through an open window landing on the fire escape. As Johnny and I scrambled down six floors on the fire escape I could hear two things, bullets ricocheting off the metal grating and steps, and Johnny laughing. The laughing stopped abruptly as we found ourselves running in mid-air off the second-floor of the fire escape. We didn't realize the escape stopped on the second-floor and you had to grab on to a latter which slowly repelled to the ground-floor.

To make matters worse we had no shoes on because when you entered the poker room every one was told they had to take off their shoes so the rug didn't get dirty. I realized that the shoe removal thing was part of the scam so you couldn't do what Johnny and I had just accomplished, hurriedly exiting the room. Here we were running over stones, glass, and other litter through Amarillo's alleyways trying to elude what we believed would be hot pursuit and possible death.

We finally reached an area far enough from the Amarillo Hotel to feel safe. Exhausted we stopped to check if we had any bullet wounds, finding that except for bleeding feet, and a few bumps and bruises from the fire escape, we were in good shape. I asked Johnny what in the world he thought was so funny when we running for our lives down the fire escape with those bullets flying by us. He started laughing again, saying "Look at this," holding out his right hand which was full of money he had grabbed off the poker table just before jumping out the window. We laughed as we walked shoeless all the way back to the base in the pouring rain. We never returned to the city of Amarillo again. Not long after the hotel incident Johnny went AWOL and ended up being caught and sent to the Brig, which is the military term for jail. We all called him Johnny AWOL (Absent With Out Leave) and sang "Johnny AWOL" to the tune of a popular song entitled "Johnny Angel." We never saw him again.

When we graduated from tech-school we were given our new base assignment. I couldn't believe it when my orders read, Laughlin Air Force Base, Del Rio, Texas. I remember laughingly commenting, "I joined the Air Force to see the world and all I was going to see was Texas."

CHAPTER 9

THE WILD WILD WEST

—⚬⚬—

B etween the time tech-school ended and the date I was ordered to report to my permanent duty station at Laughlin Air Force Base in Del Rio, Texas, I was granted a ten day leave. I couldn't wait to strut around in my dress blue uniform just as George and Willie had. It was great to have other travelers tell you to please go ahead of them in the crowded airports. However, I always thanked them for their courtesy but insisted they go ahead of me.

The attention and respect the military uniform commanded brought a sense of pride and purpose I had never experienced before. I received the same welcome when I visited the bars back home. I couldn't buy a drink, everyone wanted to cater to my every whim. The problem was that because everyone was so nice to me there was no one to fight. I had to go to the Blue Inn, a bar known as the Saturday night fight club, to engage in a good old knock-them-out-brawl. Even with the Blue Inn available for a fight or two, it just wasn't the same with out George and Willie. The ten days at home passed so rapidly it was over before I could catch my breath. Of course it is hard to catch your breath when you spend the majority of your time drinking at local bars.

The big day came; I was winging my way from Buffalo to San Antonio, where I would catch a bus to Del Rio. I didn't like to fly, well actually, flying I liked, crashing is what I didn't like. My fear of crashing stemmed from an incident when Mom, Gram, and I were flying to Florida when I was 12 years old. We were on the first leg of the journey, flying from Buffalo to Washington, when we flew through a violent storm with severe turbulence causing the plane to bounce all over the sky.

I had chosen to sit by myself in a seat two rows behind Mom and Gram. The turbulence was so strong that no one was allowed to leave their seats for any reason. I sort of enjoyed the plane rocking and rolling until Mom, with grave concern in her voice made the comment, "I hope we don't crash." From that moment on I never have enjoyed flying, though I have flown around the world.

After landing in San Antonio I caught the bus for Del Rio. There were only a few towns such as Brackettville, Hondo, and Uvalde on the entire 159-mile trip, and all looked as if they were still in the 19th Century. Each town had railroad tracks running along Main Street and wood frame buildings with false fronts to make them look larger than they actually were. Every building was bleached by the sweltering west Texas sun.

What was scary was that except for those few small towns, there was nothing but dust, tumbleweed, tarantulas, and rattlesnakes the entire way. At every bus station you could purchase rattlesnake skins, belts, shoes, and watchbands.

I remember lamenting, "What the H_ _ _ did I get my self into? If there are only these few small antiquated towns between civilianization in San Antonio and my destination, Del Rio, what would it be like?" Here I was, a young man from just outside Buffalo, New York, traveling to live at an Air Force Base in the heart of cowboy country, west Texas.

I detested country music, western attire, and anticipated a culture war.

When I arrived in Del Rio I didn't want to get off the bus, my worst nightmare was a reality; everyone wore blue jeans, cowboy hats, and boots. Most of the vehicles were pick-up trucks adorned with gun racks full of rifles and "Hook um Horns stickers," which the cab driver who took me to the Air Force base said referred to the University of Texas Long Horns Football team. Some of the pick-up trucks even had authentic horns from Texas Long Horn cattle mounted in the grill.

The barrooms along the streets all had country music blaring, and from my vantage point didn't seem like places a "dude" from New York would be welcome. The cabbie confirmed my intuition when he pointed out a sign in front of a bar stating "Dogs, Yankees, and Airman Keep Off the Grass." At that instant I was sure I had entered the Twilight Zone. I was going to spend up to three years stationed in a place full of bigoted red necks. The cabbie who was of Mexican descent, assured me that, "his people," as he pointed across the Rio Grande River to Mexico, would be much more hospitable.

Laughlin Air Force Base had one mission: training fighter pilots. There was a squadron of T-41 Piper Cub style trainers, used in the first stage of pilot training, a squadron of T-37 Jet trainers, used in second phase of pilot training, and a squadron of T-33 Jet trainers used in advanced pilot training. I was assigned to work on the T-33's.

The T-33's were antiquated trainers and with in a short time were replaced by the new T-38 dual-engine advanced trainers. The T-38 was a fabulous airplane, far out performing its predecessor, awesome to work on, and amazing to watch fly. We loved to see them roaring down the runway with both J-85 jet engines full throttle, flames streaming from their afterburners as they pulled up into a vertical climb. The aircraft was so powerful that it reached 30,000 feet in just over two minutes. Our T-38 Squadron was the pride of the base.

Because of my work ethic and prowess as a jet mechanic, I was offered a job working in *Maintenance and Test* where T-38's with major engine, hydraulic, or electrical problems were sent for repair. It was exciting to work with the other highly motivated mechanics, along with the Technical representatives from the Northrop Corporation who designed and built the T-38. We were held to an extremely high standard of proficiency in repairing the planes. If we erred in following protocols of quality control the result could spell disaster for the test pilots.

I remember a young mechanic who totally ignored protocols for reconnecting the cables that joined the control stick to the elevons which gave the airplanes their up and down movement. When Major Mapes, our most experienced and proficient test pilot, lined up on the runway, we hurried out of the hanger to watch the takeoff and maneuvers he would put the plane through. Major Mapes was an amazing pilot; always causing oohs and ahs as he barrel-rolled the plane during his vertical assent to approximately 10,000 feet, followed by other acrobatic maneuvers.

However, on this particular test flight we immediately knew he was in serious trouble. When he attempted to put the plane into his classic vertical take off climb the plane wouldn't go up, it flattened out horizontally within seconds of lift off and started to waffle violently. Listening to the radio transmissions between Major Mapes and the control tower, we immediately heard him declare an emergency as he struggled to keep the plane in the air. It was horrifying to watch the plane heading for the ground, and then suddenly veer up 200 or 300 feet in the air, then right into another 200 foot dive.

Major Mapes fought to get the crippled plane away from the base so if he had to eject it wouldn't crash into a Base housing area near the flight path. Everyone was horrified and yelling, "Eject, eject!" as it seemed certain the plane was about to crash. After what seemed like an eternity Major Mapes was finally able to gain enough control to bring the plane in for an emergency landing. As fire and emergency equipment raced toward the runway, my mind flashed back to Millgrove Bible Church and people praying for God to intercede in crisis situations. Instantly I prayed for Jesus, who I hadn't spoken to in years, to please help Major Mapes land the plane safely.

Within a few minutes, the plane bounced up off, then back down onto the runway until it safely came to a stop. Everyone on the flight line was cheering. The plane was towed to our hanger where our investigation revealed that when the young mechanic had reconnected the cables from the pilot's control stick to the elevons, instead checking the positioning of the cables according to speciation's, he changed the length of the cables by unscrewing and extending turnbuckles to make them fit. The error nearly cost Major Mapes his life. He was removed from our team and barely escaped severe disciplinary action.

Often pilots in training felt they were ready for acrobatic maneuvers long before their flying skills necessary to perform them had actually developed. This usually happened soon after they had been cleared to fly the second level T-37 Jet trainers in solo flight with out being accompanied by instructor pilots. I personally witnessed the tragic results of just such overconfidence by two young pilots.

We in *Maintenance and Test* were asked if we would volunteer to help recover the remains of two T-37's which crashed after two solo pilots had a mid-air collision while pretending to be dog fighting. "Dogfights" occur when fighter pilots perform acrobatic maneuvers to get into position to shoot down an enemy plane. Pilot training bases are located in remote, sparsely populated areas because training pilots is a dangerous business. I became keenly aware that the military didn't want their airplanes falling from the skies into residential neighborhoods when we arrived at the crash site. The vast desolate area wasn't inhabited by people, however, there were LOTS of critters to contend with, including rattle snakes, scorpions, and gigantic tarantulas.

The initial crash investigators concluded that as the pilots were maneuvering as if in a dogfight, one plane's wing clipped the other plane's wing. This resulted in one descending almost straight into the ground, followed by the other plane hitting trees and burning as the pilot attempted a crash landing. Both pilots were subsequently killed, the first on impact, the second when trapped in the burning wreckage of his plane. By the time we arrived at the crash sight, the pilot had been extracted from the burnt out wreckage of the second plane.

We were given the horrific task of digging up the remains of the first plane which crashed almost vertically into the ground. One picture haunts my memory from digging that wreckage from the crater produced upon impact; the removal of the remains of the pilot. When the World Trade Center was attacked by using planes, images from our 1965 recovery flashed through my mind.

Because I was an excellent mechanic and my participation in the crash site recovery was admirable, I became our sergeant's golden boy. He informed me I would be his choice for Airman of the month. If there was one thing I couldn't stand it was prosperity. The very day I was nominated for the award, I disqualified myself by doing what I loved to do, get drunk and fight.

After working all day, my buddies and I decided to go over the border to Mexico to have a few drinks and enjoy the floor shows in the night clubs. We returned to base at 11:30

at night and because the dining hall was open from 11:30 to 12:30 for "midnight chow," we decided to get something to eat. All went well until the short order cook who was sweating profusely, leaned over the eggs he was cooking for us. I asked him to please refrain from sweating on our eggs. He responded by reaching over the serving counter and slapping me in the face with the extremely hot, grease-covered spatula he was using to flip the eggs.

In an instant I vaulted over the counter grabbing the cook by the neck, pushing him through the kitchen doors and on to a steam table where I attempted to drown him. It took four people to pull me off him, including two Military Police (MP) who witnessed the entire incident. After wrestling to remove me from the mess hall, they attempted to put me into the Military Police pick up truck. I refused to get in the truck unless I could ride "shotgun," which meant riding next to the passenger side door. After watching me almost drown the 200 Lb cook, then struggling to get me out of the mess hall, the MP Sergeant told his assistant to get in the middle, allowing me to ride shotgun. My buddies were roaring as I waved to them out the truck window on my way to the brig.

I only wish I could report that my First Sergeant was amused by my little misunderstanding with the cook. However, he took a rather dim view of the whole episode, punishing me with a 90 day suspended bust in rank and restriction to base for 30 days. I was not one who could easily accept being restricted to our boring base, when all those Mexican honeys were waiting for me. So, true to form, I went to the back gate where one of my friends in base security let me go off the base.

Off I went to Mexico thinking it prudent to only go to nightclubs where I wasn't known, just in case our First Sergeant anticipated my escape. I went to a club just over the Rio Grande Bridge into Mexico far removed form my usual hang-outs in the more popular clubs in a section of Acuna called "Boys Town." As I moseyed up to the bar to order a drink, who do I see at a corner table, my First Sergeant in a lip lock with a prostitute! That was the end of my restriction and problems with him.

Having the open and wild environment of Mexico only eight miles from base provided a venue conducive to my life style. I could drink and fight with few repercussions, and little police intervention. However, one Friday night, one of my buddies and I were partying at our favorite bar, the "# 8 Club," when we caught a Mexican man picking pockets. The club had stage shows featuring "Sandra the Banana Woman." I won't describe why she had that name or why the other featured performer was called the "Donkey Woman," I am sure you can guess what the total perversion and abominations their stage names represented.

While the strippers were performing, the pickpocket would bump into GI's who were intently watching the show, picking their wallets out of their pockets. When the guy attempted to pick my buddies pocket we were ready for him. My buddy sliced his hand with a pocket knife and the pickpocket ran off disappearing into the night. With in ten-minutes numerous Mexican Police cars roared up to front door of the # 8 Club. Who comes out of the police car but the pick pocket that identifies my buddy as the person who cut him! It turned out that he was an off duty Cop.

In the scrum that ensued I ended up being arrested along with my buddy. We were transported to the Acuna jail where we were thrown into a filthy cell, already housing more than 20 Mexican prisoners. In the middle of the cell there was a two inch round pipe sticking up about two-feet high that was used as a toilet. Everyone slept on the dirt covered concrete floors, sharing filthy wool blankets to keep warm in the damp cell. The odors from dirty bodies and the sewer pipe were almost unbearable.

There was one prisoner, however, who everyone seemed scared of. He slept in the only bunk in the cell. I found a bilingual cellmate who explained that there were kids as young as 12 and men as old as 80 locked up for various crimes including burglary, prostitution, robbery, and murder. He also explained the social order. The poor young kids were repeatedly sodomized by the older men. The prisoner in the bunk was a murderer who was referred to as the "King of the Cell." After assessing the situation, I decided that the murderer needed to relinquish the bunk; I had no intention of sleeping on the floor.

I walked over to him, grabbed him by the neck yanking him out of the bunk, and slammed him to the floor. I proceeded to stomp him half-to-death, knocking him unconscious. When he came to, I attacked him again just to be sure he knew who the new "King of the Cell" was. When he regained consciousness the second time, I again started to kick and stomp him as he crawled to the opposite corner of the cell, curling up into a fetal position. He didn't move from that corner for the day-and-a-half I remained in the jail.

Every Sunday the Military Police secured the release of military personnel locked up during the weekend. We had to pay a $250 fine and were told that we were barred from visiting Mexico for 30 days. After experiencing the Acuna Jail we gladly stayed out of Mexico for a while. I guess they thought if they deprived us of the prostitutes and night clubs for 30 days, we wouldn't cut the hands of corrupt cops moonlighting as pickpockets.

It was nice to be able to go to Boys Town for sex with the prostitutes, however, I always was concerned with contracting a sexually transmitted disease. Consequently, I was extremely careful, frequenting the same very high priced girl the entire time I was there. I never contracted gonorrhea or syphilis like many other Airmen did. One of my friends was stricken with syphilis from a prostitute who worked in the # 8 Club. He was confined at the base hospital, receiving antibiotic injections until the infection was controlled. I couldn't believe it; as soon as he was released from the hospital, he couldn't wait to run back to the # 8 Club, having sex with the same infected girl. This time, after treatment, he was discharged from the Air Force. Many of the young service men who were 17 and 18 years old never experienced sex until visiting the prostitutes in Mexico. Things have really changed since 1964, haven't they?

After the initial few months and a handful of bad experiences, like being tossed in the Acuna jail, my friends and I seldom visited Mexico. Instead we spent most of our free time at the base bowling alley watching and flirting with the teenage daughters of the military families stationed at the base. In spite of valiant efforts to keep their daughters away from us, including, making the base teen center off limits to military personnel, we developed friendships with the teenage girls.

Our group was comprised of five airmen and five daughters of Sergeants and Officers. At times we would date, but most of the time we just hung out together at the bowling alley, pools, and the Lake Walk Military Resort located 15 miles from the base. The Lake Walk Base Resort was actually intended for use by officers, usually pilots in training, to provide a respite from the pressures of flight training.

There was a Club that doubled as a barroom and administration building from which cabins, speed boats, and water skis could be rented. The Officers seldom rented all the cabins, so there was usually one available for our weekend parties. We often rented the speedboats and would water ski the entire length of the 14 mile long lake. I spent many weekends fishing in Lake Walk and the surrounding tributaries of the Rio Grande River.

The father of one of the girls I dated, Diane, was a Staff Sergeant and a pervert, who repeatedly tried to have sex with her. He even resorted to taking us to Mexico in an attempt to get us drunk hoping then she would agree to have sex with him. He promised to buy her a car, pay for college costs, and even pay her to submit to sex. What drove him crazy was the fact that he knew Diane and I were having sex almost every day. He even tried to bribe me into convincing her to have sex with him.

It wasn't long before the weight of his perversion resulted in Diane and I breaking up, however, we did remain friends. Sadly, Diane's mother knew that her husband was attempting to seduce his own daughter but was too intimidated to report him to the Police. The only salvation for Diane was that her father was transferred to Cam Rang Air Force Base in Vietnam for a 12 month temporary duty assignment. We were hoping that he wouldn't come back, or if he did it would be in a pine box.

After Diane and I broke up, I started to date another girl from our "in-crowd," a Major's daughter named Virginia. She and I were the perfect match, soul mates that just loved to be together no matter what we were doing. We spent almost every evening and all weekend together at the base pool, at the bowling alley, or at Lake Walk making love. Her father, the Major, and I got along just great. He was an alcoholic and loved to share war stories over a few cold beers. I loved the stories, the beer, and his daughter.

Every six months we were allowed to ask for a transfer to another base. I had repeatedly requested to be transferred to Vietnam where I pictured myself becoming a war hero. Every time I requested my supervising Sergeant to approve my transfer, he would comment that I was one of the most proficient jet mechanics he ever had encountered, with a great personality, a born leader with unlimited potential, who was throwing it all away over a beer and a fight. He always lamented that if he could keep me at work on the flight line 24 hours a day I would be Airman of the year. He often asked, "Faulring, what makes you so good at work all day and so bad all night?"

He signed my transfer request saying that he would miss my good work, the excitement I provided, and sarcastically thanked me for causing him to be on a first name basis with almost all the Military Police Officers on base. Shaking his head he would ask himself, "How could a skinny runt like Faulring be such a wild animal in a fight?"

What he didn't know was that I was following a skewed version of what my Grandfather had instilled in me from the time I was a little boy, to work as hard as I could, and do the best I could at everything I did. To me that meant to work hard to be the best jet mechanic, but also be the best fighter I could be. In July of 1966 the Sergeant came to me and said "Faulring you have your wish, your going to Vietnam." I was ecstatic, I was going to be a war hero, and then maybe I would be someone worth keeping. It seemed funny but I was going to miss Del Rio. I had grown to enjoy the warm weather all year round, the people, and even the Air Force base.

When I received my orders, I also found out that our whole "in-crowd" crew had also been transferred to south East Asia. We had a tearful farewell party with our friends at Lake Walk and off we went to war.

CHAPTER 10

WORK HARD, PLAY HARDER

—ɯɯ—

Before I left for the Vietnam War I was allowed to take a 30 day leave. Those days flew by as I partied the entire time, not drawing one sober breath. If I was going to go to war and possibly be killed, I was going to make sure my last party was one to be remembered. I said goodbye to all my friends just in case I didn't come home alive. I reminded them of my philosophy from school, I was going to *live fast, die young, and have a good looking corpse.* The way I was living, it was a wonder that I hadn't already accomplished just that.

As I flew across the country to Travis Air Force Base California, my flight stopped in Chicago for a two hour layover. I went into a bar in the airport to have a few drinks while waiting for my next flight. Everyone wanted to buy the GI headed for war a drink. The bartender asked if I was 21 years old, the legal age to drink in Illinois. I wasn't, but before I could respond, a former Marine who served in World War II chastised the bartender, arguing that any boy being sent to die for his country deserved to be able to have a drink no matter what age. Everyone at the bar voiced their agreement and I was served my drink. As the people at the bar bought me drinks they would raise their glasses saying, "God Bless you! Go get those Commies and kill one for me."

When I left the bar to catch my fight to San Francisco everyone stood up and cheered as the former Marine snapped to attention saluting me. It was great! I envisioned returning home a war hero, an Audi Murphy of sorts, decorated with medals especially purple hearts for bravery. When I arrived in California the same type of welcome greeted me; people shaking my hand, wanting to buy me drinks, and commenting about how proud they were of our troops.

The flight to Southeast Asia on a chartered commercial airliner was filled to capacity with military personnel. As the plane approached Hawaii for refueling the pilot circled Pearl Harbor. From the air we could see the outlines of the ships sunk in the 1941 attack. It was a poignant moment to see Battleship Row and the Arizona's outline under the water. After resuming our flight we passed over Wake Island and Guam, which were strategic islands during World War II. I couldn't help wondering how many courageous young soldiers had lost their lives on those small islands in the middle of the Pacific Ocean. We finally landed after what seemed to be an eternity in the air. As we disembarked the plane I was immediately blasted by extreme heat. I thought, whew, this Vietnam is one hot country. What a shock it was when I found that I was in the Philippine Islands not Vietnam. Now how in the world would I become a war hero stationed at this country club of a base? They didn't give out purple hearts for getting hit by a ball on the base golf course.

The Airman's Club, called "The Coconut Grove," featured first class entertainers such as Diana Ross and the Supremes, Brenda Lee, and the Everly Brothers just to mention a few. It also housed a barber shop with manicures and pedicures available as your hair was being cut, along with a gambling room full of slot machines. Clark Air Force Base had numerous restaurants, pools, and movie theaters.

The barracks were air conditioned with snack shops serving hot sandwiches and beer. Philippine "House Boys," cleaned the rooms and did all our laundry. This place was a Southeast Asian paradise.

I was assigned to the 509th Fighter Interceptor Squadron which maintained the F-102 Fighter Jets used to scramble and intercept enemy MiG Fighter Jets, chasing them back to North Vietnam. The good thing about the 509th was that we had a detachment stationed in Bien Hoa Vietnam and there was a good possibility that I would be able to go there on temporary duty. I was ecstatic; my dream of being a war hero might still come true.

Being stationed in the Philippines was much like being in Del Rio, there was a town just out side the base called Angeles City, full of bars, clubs, and prostitutes. I remember the first time I visited Angeles City; the road side was crammed with vendors selling everything from paintings and jewelry to "Dog on a Log." Dog on a Log was actual dog legs barbequed on charcoal pits.

What made eating dog legs gross was that they came from live dogs kept in a pen along side the cooking pit. When he needed more legs to barbeque, the vender would club one of dogs over the head, knocking it unconscious. Then with a sharp knife cut the legs off and cook them. I decided to be a wise guy and asked a vendor what kind of dogs he was serving, to which he wryly replied, "Slow!"

There were two initiation rituals all new Airmen were challenged to experience upon their first trip to Angeles City. First, eating Dog on a Log, and second, eating a balot. Balots were chicken's eggs almost ready to hatch, which had been buried in the ground for 45 days. At the end of that time they were dug up and eaten, slimy feathers and all. If you were like me, you would only eat one!

In the Philippines the favorite mode of transportation was Jeepneys, which were Jeeps colorfully painted and decorated with chrome ornaments. People could ride almost anywhere in Angeles City for ten cents. Busses, which were the second most popular means of travel, were usually of World War II vintage, always fully packed with people inside, and chickens crammed on the roof.

Clark Air Force Base was located about 100 miles north of Manila, the Capital City of the Philippines. Manila, positioned on the southern tip of the Island Of Luzon, had a naturally protected bay inlet that housed Subic Bay Naval Base, the largest and most strategic naval shipyard in Southeast Asia. It was a critical naval staging area during World War II and now a critical staging area for the Vietnam War.

Angeles City, adjacent to Clark Air Force Base, and Olangapo City, which was adjacent Subic Bay, thrived on the money spent by the military personnel at the clubs and bars lining their streets. Soldiers from the many different squadrons on the bases would pick a small club that became their hangout. Each squadron would protect their Club and fight anyone who invaded their territory. It became a sport to invade other bars and have good old knock-down-drag-them-out-brawls.

For me the Empire Club in Angeles City became my territory. It wasn't long before I gained a reputation for fighting anyone who challenged my squadron, the 509[th's] claim to the bar. In fact, I was nick named "Boom-Boom" by Momma Linda who owned the Empire Club and was Madam of the club's prostitutes. Every night when I arrived at the club everyone knew that sooner or later, Boom-Boom would be fighting.

Each club had a Philippine Constabulary Police Officer paid by the owner of the bar for security and protection. The Empire Club's Constabulary's name was Johnny. Johnny and I became good friends, first, because I was a great fighter, and second because I would bring him food from the base and give him money to help support his family. We became so close that he invited me to visit his mother, father, and other relatives who lived on the southwestern end of the island of Luzon.

There was a little problem however; military personnel were restricted from traveling to that section of the Island due to the prevalence of communist insurgents known as "Hucks." Because Johnny's family lived along the coast near Santa Cruz Bay, I not only wanted to have the honor of meeting his family, but also scuba dive on a Japanese ship sunk near there during World War II. The trip was so alluring that the risks it posed seemed worth taking. I talked a friend and fellow scuba diver named Jerry into joining me in the adventure.

We took five days leave and joined Johnny for the trip to his home village, hiring a Jeepney to take us down the coast past Subic Bay, toward Santa Cruz and Huck territory. The Jeepney driver dropped us off about ten miles into Huck country, where we hired a rice farmer with an Ox cart to haul us and our scuba gear for the rest of the trip. We had to stop and wait while rice was being loaded into carts after being dried on the only path through the rice paddies. For hauling our gear the ox cart driver charged us ten pesos which was $2.50 American, about a month's wages for him. We tipped him 100 pesos ($20) to be sure he would be available and waiting for us in three days for our return trip. Johnny informed us there hadn't been an American soldier in his home village since World War II.

When we arrived the entire village came out to greet us. Johnny's family was excited to see him and to honor the American's who came with him. At first Jerry and I were a little intimidated and worried by all the mass excitement over two American Soldiers being in an area frequented by Communist insurgents.

Johnny's family's village was about 100 yards from the bay and consisted of two story bamboo huts mounted on poles. The huts were divided into four small rooms separated by bamboo walls. There was also no furniture, only mats on the floor used as beds. In one room a rather large flat rock with a small fire on it was used to cook the staples of their diet, fish, and rice.

The entire male population was fishermen. They used small, extremely narrow outriggers called Banka boats to fish, and everyone benefited from the catch which was shared by the village.

As Jerry and I donned our scuba diving gear we were filled with excitement in anticipation of diving on a sunken Japanese warship. The ships final resting place was on a reef with the bow in approximately 40 feet and stern in 100 feet of water.

The Philippine skin divers could only hold their breath long enough to dive to the bow attempting to catch Sea Bass, they called Laupu Laupu, with primitive spears. Jerry and I could easily dive to up to 100 feet, however, dove to no more than 50 feet allowing us to stay submerged longer to spear fish and also look for souvenirs. We were proficient at both.

What the fishermen in the boats above our dive wanted were big Laupu Laupu, which were easy pray for Jerry and I to harvest with our spear guns. We would spear fish and send them up to the boats by using CO_2 inflatable dive markers. The men in the Banka boats would ferry the fish to the waiting villagers.

We did have one harrowing experience on our second dive. Jerry swam into the middle of a school of tuna, spearing one of the largest ones in the tail. I kept banging my air tank with my dive knife trying to get Jerry's attention. He finally acknowledged my signal as I gave him the thumbs up sign to immediately ascend. As we broke the surface he pulled off his mask inquiring, what was the problem and why I didn't try to spear one of those monster tuna? I responded by pointing out that the "monster" tuna, including the one with his spear through its tail, were actually Barracuda! We scrambled into a Banka boat where we carefully pulled in the unhappy fish. As it thrashed around snapping jaws full of razor sharp teeth, the fisherman clubbed it to death. At the completion of our final day's dive the entire village threw a party in our honor thanking us for providing them with so many fish. The entire trip was a once in a life time experience.

We also joined the Clark Air Force Base Scuba Diving Club that often went on excursions with the Navy Seals from Subic Bay. They were gracious enough to allow us to join them as they practiced their diving and survival skills. Humbled just to be able to spend time with them, we weren't in their league and were dazzled by their stamina and proficiency. On one of the dives I ruptured a sinus cavity resulting in profuse bleeding and the end of my diving career.

As I was approaching the time where I would have a chance to go to our detachment in Bien Hoa, Vietnam, fate once again betrayed me. While working on an F-102, I released a safety bar holding the rudder to the side while replacing a defective actuator, when an Airman who was in the cockpit moved the control stick causing the rudder to crush my left hand.

The fourth and fifth knuckles were driven back into and over the bones in my hand. The injury was so severe that the doctors had to insert pins to hold the knuckles in place. In the millisecond it took that rudder to crush my hand, my dream of being a war hero and my career as a jet mechanic were crushed as well. I had a large cast on my hand and was told it would be a long time before I would ever be able to grip tools in it again. As a result of the injury, the Squadron Commander transferred me to our Administrative Squadron where I was assigned to work in the mailroom.

Having to work as a mail clerk was almost unbearable for a macho jet mechanic. We referred to the male clerical workers of the Administrative Squadron as, "breast-less

WAFs" (Women's Air Force), so working there was a fate worse than death. My only consolation was that Virginia's (Ginny) father, now a Colonel had been transferred to Clark Air Force Base and his family was now in the Philippines.

Ginny and I were soul mates again continuing right where we left off in Texas. We enjoyed each other in every way possible as friends, lovers, and socially with other couples. Ginny got a job on base as a dental assistant and because I was working in the mailroom our work schedules matched perfectly. In the evening we would either hang out at the base pool, Airman's club, her house, or go down to the Empire Club. I purchased a motorcycle which we traveled everywhere on.

On the weekends we would hook up with other military dependants and their friends to go cruising the clubs in Angeles City. Many of the clubs had bands playing so we made our rounds drinking and dancing the nights away. Because my friends and I were dating military dependants, other Airmen were jealous resulting in them trying to move in on girlfriends. This always provoked fights which I was more than glad to engage in.

I remember one such occasion when Ginny and I, along with another couple, were club hopping on a Saturday night in Angeles City. As we walked through one of our favorite clubs a very large Airman who was sitting at a table with three other guys grabbed Ginny's arm and said, "Come here Round Eye, (which was the descriptive term for an American girl) I would like to F_ _ _ you!"

In a flash I swung my arm with that cast on it as hard as I could striking him on the nose. He dropped to the floor with a thud; his nose flattened and blood pouring everywhere.

Wouldn't you know it, at that very moment the Military Police came through the door witnessing the attack. They took me into custody and back to their Headquarters on Base. Ginny called her dad who procured my release to his supervision. I was brought up on charges that resulted in a hearing to decide if I should be Court Marshaled. Unfortunately the hearing was scheduled for less than a week after the incident. Because I had re-broken my hand in the attack, the doctor encased it from my hand up to my elbow with an even bigger cast. As I rested my arm on the table, my defense attorney, a young Lieutenant commented that maybe the Hearing Officer would have mercy on me when he saw the monstrosity of a cast.

Any illusions we shared that the cast would invoke sympathy quickly vanished when the victim of my rage walked into the room. He had a metal plate covered with tape over his broken nose. His face was still badly swollen, with both eyes black and blue, even my attorney gasped. Things certainly pointed to a Court Martial. Just before the hearing was about to start I walked over to the guy and apologized for the damage to his face. To my amazement he stood up and shook my hand. He said that he would have done the exact same thing if the rolls were reversed and that the incident was totally his fault. He turned to the hearing officer and asked that all charges against me be dropped.

The Major running the proceedings tried to intimidate him by saying that if he didn't testify against me he would be brought up on charges. However, he responded to the hearing officer by quoting exactly what he said to Ginny and stated that I was justified to, "Smack him for it." At that point the hearing officer declared the proceedings closed, releasing and restoring me to duty. The ironic thing was that as we were walking out of the hearing the guy asked me where I was from. When I told him east of Buffalo, New York he paused with an astonished look on his battered face replying that he was from North Tonawanda which is just north of Buffalo.

For the remaining 11months I spent in the Philippines I tried to control the violent river of rage boiling within me.

Ginny and I traveled to Subic Bay Naval Base many times to watch the Air Craft Carriers and other ships as they came in and out of port. Because Ginny was a Colonel's daughter, we were allowed to use the officers' private beach and pub located near the anchored Air Craft Carriers. It was a majestic and magnificent site to watch the ships as they left port for Vietnam.

However, I remember seeing the Aircraft Carrier, Forrestal, limping into Port after a terrible fire that was started by a bomb from a jet fighter which accidentally exploded on the deck. One of the aircraft involved in the catastrophe was piloted by none other than U.S. Senator, John McCain.

I traveled the entire route of the Bataan Death March, stopping to read every sign posted along the way. It was amazing to stand on top of the mighty gun emplacements on Corregidor. I pictured my grandfather standing on the exact same sites in 1898, his words echoing in my mind "Bobby, you would like it in the Philippines." I did!

As the war in Vietnam continued to rage on, more and more C-130 Hercules medical evacuation transport planes arrived at Clark delivering critically injured soldiers. Some times there were as many causalities as there were wounded soldiers on board the planes. It was a sad sight to see the wounded soldiers loaded in ambulances and rushed to the hospital. Even more heartbreaking was watching the black bags filled with the bodies of their fallen comrades being loaded in trucks and transported to the mortuary for embalming and shipment to the United States. I often wondered if anyone I knew was in one of those black bags.

Just before Christmas of 1967 I became very sick ending up in the hospital with a ruptured appendix. After blood tests showed I needed emergency surgery I was taken to the surgical floor and placed on a gurney to wait my turn in the operating room. Because the surgeons were feverishly operating on gravely wounded soldiers I was placed in a side room to wait for an opening in an operating room.

After over six hours stuffed in that side room I was curled up in a fetal position so sick I couldn't talk or move. Luckily a surgical assistant happened to open the door to push an empty gurney inside and saw me. With one look at me curled up and unresponsive he grabbed the chart attached to my gurney and exclaimed that they probably killed me. He immediately pushed me into an operating room telling the tired surgeon that I had lain in the side room for over six hours with a ruptured appendix.

My system was so full of poison they didn't know if I would survive. I wasn't sure if I would survive either when I awoke in a makeshift intensive care unit set up in a Quonset hut along side the hospital. The hut was full of soldiers in critical condition; tubes sticking out everywhere, some had their heads caved in and others with arms and legs missing. It was just a horrific sight. To make things worse the temperature was hovering at over 100 degrees making the smell almost unbearable. It seemed like soldiers were dying every minute with chaplains scurrying to pray over and give last rites to many of them.

Because I was so sick from the infection and could barely talk I just laid there with tears rolling down my cheeks as I watched those valiant soldiers fight for their lives. I was ashamed to be in the same ward with those heroes and wished I could just get up and leave. During the first night I realized the Marine right next to me, whose head had been caved in so far you could have placed a basketball in it, was dying. As I heard the gurgling in his throat, I attempted to call for a nurse but was too weak to get anyone's attention. At about six a.m. they found that he was dead and removed his body. On the third day I was able to sit up and take a little nourishment. That afternoon many of us were wheeled out to the front of the hospital where Bob Hope and his team of entertainers were going to put on a Christmas show. I will never forget Anita Bryant singing the "Battle Hymn of the Republic" to those wounded soldiers, even now recalling that poignant scene sends shivers down my spine and brings tears to my eyes. After recovering enough to walk I asked to be released to my barracks for the remainder of my recuperation. When I arrived at the barracks my friends told me that my Sergeant thought I had gone AWOL, filing a missing person report. He was astonished when he found out I had been in the hospital. Ginny was worried sick and thought I had been killed somewhere off base. I had never gone more than eight hours without contacting her.

Right after my experiences with those wounded and dying soldiers, one of my best friends, Nick Masucci, was wounded at our detachment in Bien Hoa. He and two other Airmen were hit by shrapnel during a mortar attack. This was the final straw I had no chance to be a war hero and Nick had just received the Purple Heart.

Chapter 11

The Shadows Darken

—∿∿—

In April of 1968 my tour in south East Asia was over, I was finally coming home. It was exciting yet somewhat depressing; I never got my chance to be a war hero and was leaving my soul mate. However, I was excited to be returning to my family and friends. Willie was out of the Air Force while George had just 30 days left to serve at Mather Air Force Base in Sacramento, California. We had it all planned, I along with two other buddies, would stay in California until George was discharged. Once he was out, we would drive cross country stopping in Las Vegas, Texas, Florida, Maryland, and New Jersey before returning to western New York.

While I hadn't realized my desire to be a war hero, at least I worked in direct support of the war and was returning with my hero buddy, Nick. He was joining us for the trip across the country so we could personally deliver him to his family in Irving, New Jersey. We anticipated a joyous welcome home, much like the send off almost two years earlier.

In early 1967 we were winning the war, pounding North Vietnam including, Hanoi, with saturation bombing by our B-52 Bombers. Our troops never lost a battle and were on the verge of what the top allied General, William Westmorland, predicted would be a collapse of North Vietnam's will to keep fighting. What General Westmorland didn't realize was that in early 1968 President Johnson and Secretary of Defense McNamara would bow to political pressure and end the bombing of Hanoi.

I remember reading an article where one of North Vietnam's Generals revealed that if the bombing of Hanoi would have continued for three more weeks, they would have conceded that the war was lost. They would have pulled their troops out of South Vietnam so we would stop bombing Hanoi. He also made reference to the political and social groundswell of the American anti-war movement as a catalyst for rejuvenating their will to keep fighting.

We received a personal taste of the groundswell of that movement when we landed in San Francisco April 20th 1968. The same people who were cheering us when we left in 1966 were now carrying signs protesting the war. They called us "baby killers," and spit in our faces. To this day I can vividly see the long haired protesters carrying American flags upside down, burning them in the street, and even wearing them as jackets.

I wondered what the World War II veterans thought when they saw their beloved flag so defiled. I also remember thinking that we should join with the World War II Vets and go kick these anti-American, flag defiling, communist supporting traitor's blankety blank butts. How could our country allow this treasured symbol, soaked with the blood of patriots who sacrificed their all, to be dishonored in just two short years? It was mind boggling.

There was a part of the so called "Social and Sexual Revolution" that seemed exciting to me. Women burning their bras and carrying signs "Make love not war." Okay, now let me get this right, the women now wanted to have sex and call it love, and then *not* hold me responsible for the consequences? *Please sign me up right away!* I thought this might be an aberration affecting the ultra liberal San Francisco area which was light years ahead of the rest of America when it came to outrageous thought and behavior.

What soon became apparent was that this was a nation-wide plague. However, what I also realized was that there could be some great fringe benefits from this "Sexual Revolution and Awakening," whose mantra was free love, free sex, and no responsibility or consequences. There seemed to be many movements, some good, some overdue, some not so good, and some disastrous, all thrown into a melting pot called the "Social Revolution." This movement challenged every norm, value, moral pillar, and religious foundation of American culture.

There were social institutions that certainly needed to be scraped, segregation for the first one. Black Americans were virtually still slaves in many States with their lives bound by laws preventing such fundamental rights as voting, eating in restaurants, staying at hotels, getting a drink from a public water fountain, or using public rest rooms.

Black Americans volunteered to serve their country and distinguished themselves in war only to be denied their rights and recognition for their patriotic sacrifices. I had just served with many such fine young men. One reason I was accepted and respected by the African-American Airmen I served with in the Philippines, was because I never judged them, or looked at them as being inferior in any way. It was always a pleasure to join them in a brawl or two against those bigoted idiots who disrespected them because of their race. While I didn't experience anything close to the prejudice my Black friends experienced, I did understand what it was like to be treated differently because of social status. I had been fighting that battle throughout my life. We had a great time on our cross country trip. We traveled from Sacramento to San Bernardino to visit my cousin Doris who now lived there. Then it was on to Las Vegas for a day of partying and gambling. From Las Vegas we traveled to Texas to visit one of my friends, Butch, who had been a roommate in our barracks in the Philippines.

Butch was originally from North Dakota, a real life cowboy and Rodeo fan. We were about as opposite culturally as any two people alive, however, became great friends. Butch always mocked me because I played golf saying that he wasn't stupid enough to hit those little white balls then chase them all over the place. I continuously tried to convince him to try golfing just once, all to no avail. Nevertheless, fate dealt me the upper hand when we were playing poker one night in the barracks. I won $250 from him and offered to forgive the debt if he joined me for one round of golf. He reluctantly agreed.

The following Saturday we went to the base golf course for his, "One and only time chasing that stupid little golf ball around." Because the golf course Tee-times were continually full, only foursomes were allowed to play. As Butch and I waited for another two people that would join us, a Colonel and his wife came to the Tee-off area and asked if they could join us. I explained that I wasn't very good, Butch was on his first golf outing, and that we would certainly hold them back. However, the Colonel anxious to start playing, insisted.

What Airman is going to refuse a Squadron Commander? The first Tee was set on the top of a 25 foot high embankment. The Colonel's wife Teed off, driving a very nice shot down the fairway. The Colonel drove his Tee shot long and right down the center of the fairway. I let Butch go next. He missed the ball three times before hitting it to the edge of the top of the embankment followed by at least six shots to get down the embankment. I hit a fairly long and straight shot down the fairway. The Colonel, his wife, and I were on the green in three shots. It took Butch at least ten more shots to get near the green then eight putts to get in the hole.

The second hole ended up in much the same fashion with the three of us waiting while Butch half-putted his way to the green. By this time the Colonel's wife was getting impatient and cranky with us. She seemed like a real miserable witch so I was anticipating her wrath to erupt on Butch at any moment. On the very next hole, the Colonel drove the fairway; however, his wife drove her Tee shot into the right ruff. I respectfully tried to persuade her to wait until Butch Teed off before proceeding toward her ball. However, she sarcastically commented that Butch hadn't hit a Tee shot over four feet, and proceeded to walk in the ruff toward where her shot landed.

I let Butch Tee off so I could give him a few pointers on his swing. Wouldn't you know it, the first Tee shot he actually hit fairly well was heading directly at the Colonel's wife! About the time I yelled "Four," his ball hit her squarely in the butt. In an instant she grabbed her behind screaming in pain as she ratcheted her head around glaring at Butch. As Butch's eyes met mine he groaned, "I just hit the Colonel's wife in the A_ _, I'm dead."

Now here I was watching the Colonel's wife hop up and down, screaming as she was holding on to her butt. I fought to keep my composure, NOT! I fell on the ground laughing almost as hard as I am right now recalling the scene. The Colonel's wife was last seen cutting cross lots off the golf course swearing and moaning in pain all at once. About the time I stopped laughing long enough to get a glimpse at the Colonel, there he was laying on the ground, roaring himself. He got up, shook Butch's hand, and laughingly thanked him for accomplishing what he never could, getting that B_ _ _ _ of a wife of his, away from his golf game.

The course had refreshment stands every fourth hole which served soft drinks, beer, and whiskey. We stopped at everyone for the entire 18 holes. By the time we completed the round Butch had lost every one of his golf balls and all but one of mine in the water hazards or rough. The Colonel told us he hadn't had such a good time in many years inviting us to join him again any time we wanted to, an invitation we never took him up on.

After we left Texas we traveled to Alabama to see George's girl friend for a few days, and then went on to Florida for a little relaxation at Ft. Walton Beach. From there we drove up the east coast dropping a friend off in Maryland, then on to personally deliver Nick to his anxiously waiting family in New Jersey. Since New York City was right around the corner, we couldn't resist taking a bite out of the Big Apple before heading home to good old western New York on the last leg of the trip.

When we arrived home, George and I partied for two weeks before we decided to apply for a job at the Chevrolet plant in Buffalo. Being Air Force Veterans I thought we both would be snapped up but I was the only one they hired. Within a few weeks George decided to re-enlist in the Air Force and away he went. Willie had already moved to Indianapolis with his brothers to open a meat market so there I was alone again.

Because I made such good money at Chevrolet, $3.07 per hour, I decided to purchase the car of my dreams a 1967 Corvette convertible. Each night after work, I would drink my way back home stopping at the bars along the way, and spent weekends cruising around picking up girls.

As winter approached I parked my Vet and bought a beat up Chevy Nova to drive back and forth to work. One night as I was driving home form work, a police car with its emergency lights flashing and siren blaring pulled me over. As I rolled down my window to ask what the problem was, the young police officer stuck his gun in my face and told me not to move at all or he would shoot me.

I was stunned and tried too ask the officer what in the world was going on, to which he replied, "Shut up and keep your hands on the steering wheel." At that point my temper boiled over and I quickly grabbed the gun out of his hand and pointed it at him. He just about passed out and was shaking like a leaf. I walked him over to his police car and had him call for his supervisor on his police radio. I had him tell his supervisor that I had taken his gun away form him.

Not only did his supervisor respond to the radio call, almost every police officer within five miles arrived at the scene. As the Police jumped from their cars and drew down on me I asked his supervising sergeant to come to take possession of the officer's gun because he shouldn't be sticking it in my face. He refused but asked me to throw the gun to the ground and release his officer which I did.

Within seconds police officers knocked me to the ground kicking, punching, and handcuffing me. I was thrown into the back seat of a police car and deposited in a jail cell. One of the police officers at the jail informed me that a liquor store had been robbed and they were looking for a car that fit the description of mine. However, he did state that maybe the rookie police officer who stopped my car overreacted a little because the robbery victim described the perpetrators as two black males in their 20's who fled in a green Chevrolet Nova.

I knew I would need a good lawyer when the charges included assault on a police officer and reckless endangerment with a weapon. I called my cousin Richard asking if he knew a good lawyer for such a case. He gave me the name of one of the top criminal attorneys in Buffalo. I contacted the attorney who guaranteed he could get the case dismissed, however, I would have to come up with $2,000 as a retainer and another $1,000 at the end of the case.

The only way I could come up with the money was to borrow it from my dad until I could sell my Corvette to pay him back. The day my case was scheduled in court the lawyer told me to sit in a side room while he talked to the Judge. He was in the judge's chambers for 25 minutes then came out and told me not to ask any questions, informing me the case had been dropped, and everything ordered to be expunged from the court and my records. A little over a year later I found out how my lawyer persuaded the judge to dismiss my charges, when the headlines in the newspaper read, "Judge Indicted on Bribery Charges."

My life became a vicious circle of repetitious work, drinking, and fighting, causing me to burn out in less than a year. One afternoon darkness like a pall came over me and I walked out of that factory, and dropped out of the rat race I called a life.

I got a job tending bar at the Blue Inn Club in Akron, New York. It was a perfect match, I loved to fight, and working there provided ongoing opportunities to participate in one brawl after another. We were constantly either breaking up fights or right in the middle of them, it was wonderful. While working at the Blue Inn I gained a reputation as being a fighting maniac. One early afternoon as the owner Stan Baron and I were playing pool after cleaning and restocking the beer coolers, four local guys came in the bar.

I didn't know any of them however Stan was well aware of who they were and their reputation for causing trouble every where they went. Stan commented, "Here comes trouble." As Stan went to get the beer they ordered I remained at the pool table waiting for him to return so we could finish our pool game. One of the guys came over and inserted a quarter in the pool table telling me my game was over and that they were taking over the table. I said "Excuse me but Stan and I still have a game to finish." At that moment my peripheral vision caught the motion of a pool stick coming toward the side of my head.

As the pool stick struck my head I instinctively knew that if I fell to the floor I would be severely stomped by all four guys. I summoned every ounce of strength I could muster from the depths of my soul to regain my faculties and equilibrium then proceeded to attack all four of them. I knocked the closest one out cold with one left hook to his nose which also splattered it all over his face. For a mille second I pictured the Airman in the Philippines whose nose splattered the same way. I knew he was down for the count. From that moment on the entire scene was a blur of rage as I beat, kicked, and mauled the other three guys. By the time Stan had retrieved a shotgun he kept in the kitchen, I had already chased old broken nose and one other guy to a side door, as the other two fled through the front door.

Stan stood there with his shotgun in his hands, shaking his head in amazement and asking how a skinny guy like me could wreck four local hoodlums. I told him I wasn't sure but would like a beer and also to finish our pool game. Stories about that that fight circulated everywhere, elevating my reputation to epic proportions.

Because the Blue Inn was only a mile from the Tonawanda Indian Reservation many of the people who frequented it were young Seneca Indians. I became friends with many of them through fighting with or joining them in fights. I often went to drink at their homes after the Blue Inn Closed at three a.m., and gladly joined in what they called "sessions," which were actually two or three day drinking binges. We would drink whiskey, beer, and "Yagee," the Seneca name for hard cider.

Many of my friends warned me that I was nuts to hang out with those crazy Indians because a lot of them hated white people. They were sure I would be at the very least beaten profusely or even worse, killed. The funny thing was that I never thought about or cared what would happen I just enjoyed partying and fighting with the Indians.

The Indians had nick names for everyone, for example: Sanford Jonathan was called Dude, Nolan Ruben was called Chuch, Le Roy Stafford was called Kabooby, Henry Printup was called Bouncy, and Grant Sundown was called Moogie. If a guy had a girlfriend she was called "his woman," and a girl's boyfriend was called "her man." You didn't mess with another person's "man" or "woman." Many of the Indian women were great fighters and fought men and women alike.

One of the Indian families I became close friends with was known for their reputation as wild and tough. The mother, Eloise, was as tough as nails and sported a very large scar across her face and nose to prove it. She could out-drink and out-fight most men, however, she didn't have to rely solely on her fighting prowess because she had seven children with reputations of their own. One of her sons had been killed in Vietnam and another in a motorcycle accident. She had a white man named Joe who had been living with her for quite some time.

The first time I was invited to their house for a drinking party after the Blue Inn closed, Joe thought I was trying to move in on Eloise and ground a lit cigarette into the back of my neck. I jumped up quickly and beat the tar out of him. I wasn't interested in Eloise, however, her daughter Brenda, who was very beautiful, certainly caught my eye. Her oldest son Butch was a member of the KingsMen Motor Cycle Gang which had a chapter in Buffalo and another in Lockport, New York. Butch belonged to the Lockport Chapter so we often went there to hang out at a bar called the Tri-Way to drink, fight, and party.

There were a group of us who hung out at and partied with Eloise's clan. They included: Little Joe who was also in the KingsMen and his Indian woman Diana, Bouncy, and his white woman Sharon, Shelly, Brenda's friend, and me. We would often go bar hopping taking Eloise, Joe, Eloise's mother, Elysina, and her man Lenny with us.

Lenny would get so drunk he would often fall off the barstool hitting his head on the floor. To prevent injuries from falls we put a motorcycle helmet on him. The Indians called bar hopping, "Going down the line," which meant starting at the Blue Inn, we would go to each bar in the line of five bars on Bloomingdale road all the way to the Village of Akron. We also stopped at each bar on the way back to the reservation. Because I was a good fighter and always hanging out with Butch and his family, he wanted me to join the KingsMen. And so I turned the page on another chapter in my life, and headed into an even darker time.

CHAPTER 12

BIKERS, BABES, AND BLOODSHED

—ᠾᠾ—

I joined the KingsMen motorcycle gang because of its outlaw mentality which legitimized outrageous and counterculture behavior. There were guys from the Indian Reservation area that wanted to join the gang so we were allowed to start an Akron Chapter referred to as the Indian Chapter. Butch was elected President, with Little Joe as Vice President, and I became Sergeant at Arms. Eventually I became Vice president when Butch decided to leave the gang.

Life within a motorcycle gang was filled with excitement, danger, and perversion. There were battles with rival gangs, constant police harassment, sexual perversion, assaults, and murder. Some of the members of the gang were treacherous and extremely violent, willing to cut your heart out just for fun. However, there were also a lot of wanna-bes who used the gang for protection and to act tough when in reality they were really punks. The danger usually involved fights with other gangs however, you never knew where or how danger lurked.

One of my best friends from the Buffalo Chapter, who everyone called "Jug," was addicted to heroin causing him to do some very bazaar things. We were driving back from a night at the horse race track when I stopped at a red light only to have Jug jump out of the car, run over to a motel parking lot, start kicking out windows of cars, and opening the trunks to see if there was anything he could steal and sell for heroin. I drove into the parking lot, grabbed him by the neck, and threw him into the back seat of the car and sped off hoping that no one got my license plate number. You could always tell when Jug was having a "Jones," which meant he was in withdrawal, and in desperate need of more heroin to stop the physical and psychological symptoms of the body and mind craving the drug.

You would see him carrying chairs, tables, televisions, radios, and almost anything else he could get his hands on to sell at the a pawn shop and head downtown to buy drugs. I would skin pop a little heroin every now and then and also mainlined a few times, meaning injecting the drug directly into my veins with a hypodermic needle. However, I just refused to let myself be trapped into being a junkie like Jug and some of my other friends. One day Jug mainlined some very potent heroin and died with the needle in his arm. Dying from drug overdoses was just not limited to guys like Jug. Celebrities like Janice Joplin, Jim Baluchi, and Jimmie Hendrix were also tragic victims. This was the era of, "Tune in, turn on, and drop out," I guess they should have included, "And also have an extremely good chance of dying!"

The Bible talks about the consequences of repeatedly turning your back on God's Word, conviction, and refusing to repent, loving sin and perversion more than righteousness, the fruit of which is being given us over to a reprobate mind. I was consumed by a reprobate mind ignoring my Mother's and Grandmother's pleas to get out of the lifestyle I was living which they knew would eventually lead to disaster. They implored me to come back to Jesus.

What they didn't understand was the counterculture of a motorcycle gang was a blatant symbol of my rejection of everything they and society held dear, including Jesus. I was downright furious at God for allowing my Christian Father to abandon me and my Mother to marry a non-Christian who she ends up divorcing. I also was rebelling from what I considered the hypocrisy of always talking about Jesus but never attending church while loving working and shopping more than the things of God, why would I want to return to that?

Let me recant, Grandma lived a life totally dedicated to Jesus Christ bearing the fruit of repentance and had been the only stable influence in my life. In fact, when I would take my fellow gang members along with our club momma's and prostitutes to Grandma's house in the middle of the night amazing things happened. Here we were half-drunk and high on drugs, and what would Grandma do: welcome us in as if we were her long lost children. She would cook a middle of the night feast fit for a king. After we were done chowing down on eggs, bacon, sausage, pancakes, and toast, she would ask if she could have five minutes of our undivided attention. Of course everyone agreed to listen as they thanked her for the meal. Well, thanked her in the gang member and whores vernacular, "Granny your F_ _ _ing cool, yah, H_ _ _ yes Granny rap on, you're far out, your better to me than my own F_ _ _ing Mother."

Taking all these compliments in stride she proceeded to get her torn and tattered Bible, reciting Roman's road to salvation. She would tell them that she didn't care for their lifestyle, dress code, or personal hygiene but because Jesus loved them enough to die for them just as they are, she "loved them in Him!" No one ever received Christ at Gram's evangelical outreach in her dining room at 3:00 in the morning. However, God knows the seeds only she could plant in what society would describe as dregs, scum, and people who anyone else would have called the Police on if they came to their door. Rest in peace Gram, you were more than a good and faithful servant.

For the little over year-and-a-half I was a gang member, I witnessed every kind of perversion and sexual depravity imaginable: kidnapping, rape, assault, attempted murder, and a host of other crimes, it is still hard to believe I survived. I know that only the hand of God prevented me from being arrested, killed, or ending up in prison for life. I will give a few examples that only touch the surface of such darkness. I must share that it is extremely painful to recount and realize that I had spiraled down to be such a low form of humanity that I enjoyed such filth, depravity, and sin. Thank you for your mercy and forgiveness Jesus.

The gang was continually looking for girls to sexually exploit and use as "Club Momma's," to meet our appetite for sexual perversion. There were two primary targets for this purpose, first, the runaway, a girl usually between the ages of 15 and 18 whose home life often included a recent divorce. In the aftermath of the destruction of their families they would run away as a protest of their pain and fate.

Because the gang provided security and an identity of rebellion and rejection of the social structure and family that recently shattered their lives, they became easy prey. They also, in a twisted psychological paradigm, received identity reinforcement by the attachment resulting from the bond created during sex even if it was all with members of the gang.

One run away girl is a classic example. The girl's family was dysfunctional and she escaped by running away from North Tonawanda to the streets of Buffalo's west side. Two of our gang members spotted her and brought her to a bar we hung out at. We lived in a rented apartment attached to the back of the bar and offered her a place to live if she wanted to join our group. She gladly accepted the invitation. The first night only one guy had sex with her.

The next morning I asked her if she would have sex with me and of course she agreed. That night she was made to perform sexual favors for anyone who stayed at the apartment. With in a week she was a club momma, proud to be used to perform sex acts with anyone in the gang. Within a few more weeks she was used for group sex with whoever we designated including anyone who attended the parties we often threw. When she married one of the gang members and they had a child, she was still used for group oral sex.

The other target was the young girls who, because of their innocence and vulnerability, were coaxed into believing they would have a good time partying with the gang, and that we would protect them from any harm. They would be brought to a party and given alcohol, marijuana, or other drugs then attacked, gang sodomized and repeatedly raped. They were warned that if they reported what happened to them, they and their family would be murdered.

Some of these girls were never seen again others returned to become gang mommas. If our old lady, which was the term for a girlfriend, or a club momma, became pregnant, we would just take them for abortions. I am guilty of the blood of many babies murdered at abortion mills, one in the eighth month of a pregnancy. Abortion is not just a woman's issue; it is also very much a man's issue.

There were times when unsuspecting girls would make the unfortunate mistake of coming into contact with gang members purely by accident. One time this happened to a girl who lived down the street from the house Jug's sister and her lesbian girlfriend rented, who stopped by to see Jug's sister. Jug's sister wasn't home however, Jug and three other KingsMen were. They forced the girl to perform a strip tease act, after which she was repeatedly raped.

She was threatened with death if she told anyone about the attack however, she told her boyfriend who charged into the house blasting away with a 22 caliber pistol. He was shot by one of our gang members during the ensuing gun battle and then thrown off the porch into the street where he crawled back to his girlfriend's apartment. One of the neighbors who heard the commotion and gunshots called the police who couldn't get anyone to acknowledge that there had been any problem whatsoever. When Jug's sister and her girlfriend returned home, they flipped out due to the damage in the house caused by the shoot out.

I often stayed at Jug's sister's house to party for a few days. As soon her lesbian lover left to buy groceries, Jug's sister would drag me upstairs where we would have sex. What was interesting was that a girl who lived next door to our apartment on the west side of Buffalo, who also lived in a lesbian relationship with her butch partner that worked at the steel mills in Lackawanna, would invite me over for sex at least once a week. When the landlord who owned the house on College Street that Jug's sister rented, attempted to evict them, Jug and his brother burnt the place to the ground.

One of the most dangerous and perverted members of the gang was a guy named Tommy who studied karate, married a club momma, and instigated most of the parties, orgies, and fights for the gang. He eventually served over 25 years in Attica Prison for stabbing his wife's brother, a rival gang member, to death. I liked Tommy, however, I came within an instant of shooting him after he used my old lady for group oral sex at a bar on the east side of Buffalo without my permission. I know it was God's hand that kept me from shooting him because as I reached to pull out the gun it stuck in my belt and I just walked away from our altercation.

To try to explain how depraved Tommy could be is almost impossible however, this example will give you a picture. Tommy and few other gang members were partying all night and decided they needed a woman to feed their sexual appetites. There was no club mommas around so Tommy kidnapped a beautiful secretary on her way to work at a bank in the busiest section of downtown Buffalo. He forced her to take amphetamines, referred to as "speed," drink beer and wine as he and other gang members continuously raped and sodomized her for almost two days.

What was amazing was that after the two day nightmare the girl was just dropped off back on Main Street as if nothing had happened. They threatened her with death if she told anyone what they had done to her. However, after trying to hide why she missed work and didn't come home for two days, she finally broke down and told the terrifying story of her brutal attack. As she described her assailant and kidnapper the Buffalo Police knew exactly who the perpetrator was: Tommy.

I wasn't aware of the abduction and rape when I received a call from Tommy asking if I could pick him up on the west side of Buffalo and take him out to hide out at Old Man Rooney's house because he needed to "lay low for a while." We often hid out at Rooney's house drinking and partying with the Old Man when things were hot in Buffalo. After I picked Tommy up at a west side bar I asked if he wanted to stop at the Tudor Lounge in down town Buffalo before heading out of town. A few drinks later, we both needed to use the men's room. Just as I was about to flush the urinal I felt a gun against the back of my head with a cop yelling for me to place my hands in the air and not to move or he would "Blow your F—ing head off!" I slowly raised my hands over my head which were immediately slapped with hand cuffs. As I was being frisked I was glad I had accidentally left my illegal gun along side of the seat in my car.

I looked around and shuttered as I saw at least six members of the Buffalo Tactical Police Force with guns drawn on Tommy as he was being cuffed. We were dragged outside where I was asked for identification which the police used to check to see if I was a wanted man. After they determined that I had no outstanding warrants, they released me and I immediately hightailed it out of the city.

The most sickening thing was that Tommy was sentenced to just one year in County Jail after pleading to a reduced charge with the kidnapping and rape charges being dismissed. The reason for the plea reduction to a misdemeanor was that the victim did not want to go through a Jury Trial, be in the same room with Tommy, let alone have to testify about and relive the horror of her ordeal.

It wasn't very long before I found myself in the position of needing to get out of town for a while. The police were cracking down on gangs and the narcotics squads were raiding all my friends' apartments. There was also an irate father of a girl who claimed that I had made his daughter pregnant and was trying to find me. I decided to take a trip to Houston Texas to stay with my old friend George Rooney and his wife until things cooled down in western New York.

George worked at the Houston Space Center altitude chambers training Astronauts. It was a good thing I left New York when I did because with in a few weeks after my departure, our KingsMen Club House in Lockport was raided with many of my close friends being busted. With things being so hot in New York I decided to find a job in the Houston area so I could put some time between all the raids and drug busts before returning home.

I found employment as an encyclopedia salesman. The pay wasn't very good but there were numerous fine young ladies working for the company. Because I was fairly tall, had blond hair, blue eyes, and possessed a charismatic personality I was on the "hot" list of the young ladies on our sales team. They invited me to the weekend parties where I had my choice of who I would go home with. The fact that I was the hottest guy at work didn't set well with the locals. Here was this "Yankee from New York," cutting in on the homegrown Texas gent's territory. One Saturday night four of those local gents decided that it was time for the Yankee to be "taken down."

One of the guys challenged me to a fight which I was more than glad to accommodate. However, just as I connected a left hook to the jaw of the guy challenging me, knocking him to the floor, I caught a glimpse of something coming toward my head. In an instant I was knocked to my knees by the object which turned out to be the portable record player. I struggled to get to my feet as I was repeatedly kicked and knocked through a door way and out into a parking lot.

I gained my balance and landed another left-hook to the jaw of the first guy out the door and he went down. However, at that point my luck ran out, the other three guys tackled me and began kicking me with their very pointed and hard leather cowboy boots. I attempted to crawl away but the biggest guy pounced on my back, holding me down as one of the other guys bit large chunks of skin and tissue out of my back. Years later, my wife would be horrified when she saw the teeth outlined scars and felt the craters of missing tissue under them.

That was the end of my encyclopedia sales job. I found new employment working a day labor job loading barges in Houston bay. I was such a good worker the barge company tried to convince me to apply for permanent employment, however, I was burnt out on Texas, and the call to get out on the road was heavy on my mind.

CHAPTER 13

THE LONG ROAD HOME

A s I planned my exit from Texas one of the other
employees, Jerry, who worked with me loading barges,
asked where I was planning to go. I told him I wasn't sure
but Florida seemed like a good destination. He asked if he
could join me for the trip. I thought about the pros and cons
of his request and realized that it was harder for two guys
to hitchhike a ride; however, much safer. Since I would be
hitchhiking through Louisiana, Mississippi, and Alabama
in 1969, with my extremely noticeable New York accent,
having a guy with a Texas drawl with me seemed like an
intelligent option.

My intuition proved fruitful the very first day on the
road. George dropped us off at an interstate highway heading
east toward Louisiana. As we walked along hitchhiking a
car came by numerous times. It would pass us and then a
few minutes later we would see it on the other side of the
highway going by as the driver stared intently at us. The
fourth time around the car stopped and the driver inquired as
to our destination.

We immediately recognized that he was a homosexual
by his feminine voice and body movements. We told him we
were heading to Florida. He said he was only going about 20

miles but we could at least get down the road that far. I was going to tell (using the vernacular of 1969) the "fag" to get lost. However, we were a little chilly and had been walking for a few hours so we jumped in the car. Jerry rode in the front passenger seat and I was in the back seat right behind him.

Within minutes the driver started to tell us how his boyfriend had this "very large one" and that they were always looking for guys to party with. He asked if we would like to go to his boyfriends place to party. At that moment Jerry felt the guy trying to rub his leg and instantly batted his hand away and ordered him to pull the car over. When the car stopped, Jerry slapped him along side the head as we jumped out. We laughed as we walked along recounting how the guy talked and acted like a girl. Little did we know that the guy and his homosexual partner would be arrested for drugging, raping, and murdering hitchhikers!

When we got into Louisiana we received a ride from a genuine "good-old-boy" red neck, driving a 1952 Chevrolet pickup truck. I let Jerry do most the talking only responding with a few short, "Yups'" and "Na's" in response to the their conversations, I certainly didn't want him to hear my accent.

I started to doze off and didn't even realize the truck had turned off the four lane highway on to a narrow two lane road. Every thing seemed fine as we lazily rolled along with Jerry and the red neck exchanging stories. I was suddenly aroused when the driver in a laughing sort of tone said, "End of the line boys." It sure was the end of the line, we were stranded in a small hamlet in God only knows where, Louisiana.

As we surveyed our surroundings we saw a building housing a combination gas station, garage, and small grocery store. There was also a wooden building adjacent to the gas station which by the twangy country music reverberating from within, was obviously the local watering hole. I figured we were in deep trouble when I saw all the pick-up trucks and old run down cars parked beside them all sporting rebel flags. The place could have easily been the setting for a Dukes of Hazard movie.

There were railroad tracks about 200-yards from the bar with almost the identical buildings on the other side of them. The only difference was that those buildings were in worse condition than the run down ones we were standing by. It was mid-day, extremely humid with temperatures well into the 90's.

When the music in the bar stopped we could hear the high pitched sounds made by thousands of locusts. I remember asking Jerry how in the world did we end up there and even more pressing, how in H_ _ _ were we going to get out of there? We knew one thing for certain; very few if any cars were passing through this twilight zone. As we contemplated our options I came to the realization that we were in a very scary predicament. I was parched, desperately needing a drink of water, we had no money, and even worse I had to go to the bathroom.

I tried to ignore both excruciating needs for as long as humanly possible. However, there came a time when I was out of options, I had to go into that redneck bar in the middle of no where Louisiana which surely would be filled with KKK members. Remember, this was in the height of the civil rights movement, 1969 and Yankee Civil Rights activists were being murdered in the south.

As I entered the joint everyone turned to stare at me as the bartender asked, "Can I help ya boy?" I pointed to the men's room sign hoping to be able to use it before they realized that I was a Yankee. As I entered the dirty and smelly men's room I was horrified when I saw that there was no toilet paper. I sure wasn't going to ask the bartender for a new roll, so I did my business, pulled up my pants and hoped for the best. On the way out I approached the bar and with my best southern drawl imitation asked if I could have a drink of water. It became instantly obvious that my southern drawl was a complete failure when a good old boy sitting at the bar made the astute observation that I sounded like a G_ _ _ D_ _ _ _ Yankee!

The bartender echoed the same sentiments and told me to get my dirty Yankee, N_ _ _ _ _ loving A_ _ out of his establishment. I instantly complied heading for the door, as Jerry, who was at that moment coming in to see where I was, did an about face and out we went. I told Jerry that I was so parched and dehydrated I didn't care about any redneck rebels I had to get a drink of water no matter where I got it. As I headed to the place on the other side the tracks, Jerry quickly asked if I knew that I was going into a "colored place?" Given my most recent encounter he didn't think it was a good idea to go over there. But I didn't care, I desperately needed water.

As I walked the two hundred yards or so to the colored side of the tracks, I couldn't help but vividly remember my trips to Florida as a young boy. My mind flashed back to restaurants with signs prohibiting colored people from entering. I also remembered the public restrooms marked white men, white women, and then one restroom marked colored. However, what I recalled most vividly was the drinking fountains marked white only.

I pictured myself entering that colored bar as parched as I was, only to be told the water was for colored only. As I entered the bar I remember thinking, "Well Bobby boy you are about to find out." By the time I took two steps inside I realized that the men inside were as shocked as I was. You could have heard a pin drop, no one made a sound. With my throat even more dry and parched by the situation at hand I choked out the words; "Excuse me could I possibly have a drink of water?" The man behind the bar tilted his head and after an inquisitive stare, took a large bottle of water out of a refrigerator and poured a glass full. He then asked me to please drink it as fast as possible and get out of the place because he didn't need "No troubles."

After being in that redneck bar across the tracks I realized what he meant. I chugged down the water and thanked him with a quick salute as I hurried out the door. I walked over to Jerry who had been impatiently keeping a vigilance to see if anyone saw me enter the colored bar. We started to half jog back over the tracks to get out of there as fast as possible. I didn't take long in the sweltering heat before exhaustion slowed our pace.

A few cars and pick-up trucks passed us by as we attempted to hitchhike our way back toward the interstate highway. About a half-hour after we were out of the little hamlet along came a car with two black guys in it. I recognized them from the bar. They stopped and hesitantly asked if we wanted a ride. We asked where they were going and they replied New Orleans. New Orleans sounded tantalizing; however, I asked if they could drop us off at the nearest main highway that headed toward Florida. As the driver replied, "Yes Sir," Jerry and I looked at each other, shrugged our shoulders, and jumped in the back seat of their car. They said they realized I was from the north by my accent and wanted to know if I was a Civil Rights worker. I told them I was from New York but not a Civil Rights worker.

It was difficult to communicate due to their Louisiana style southern drawl and my New York accent, but they were curious to learn about New York and what I was doing in Louisiana. I explained that I was traveling from Texas to Florida and then back to New York letting some time to pass by before I returned there due to a few disagreements with our County Sheriff's Department, the City of Buffalo Police Department, and at least one cantankerous father.

Just about the time I felt semi comfortable riding with colored guys in Louisiana, the car veered down a dusty side road. At that instant the thought of being murdered and buried in a swamp, in a place where no one would ever know we had been, flashed through my mind. As I instantly reached for the knife in my back pocket the driver pulled into a driveway and up to a tattered, tin roofed, sun bleached, unpainted one-story wooden shack.

The driver announced that he had to pick up a "jug" for the trip. Sure enough he ran into the house and came out with a bottle of cheap whiskey, jumped back in the car and away we went. When we arrived at the causeway which led to New Orleans Jerry and I decided to head to Florida. We thanked the guys for the ride and whiskey as we got out of the car. After sleeping under a bridge in Mobile Alabama we began hitching a ride toward Florida the next morning. We were smelly, unshaven, and extremely hungry. In short, we were a mess!

We thumbed the whole day and only made it about 50 miles east of Mobile. It was getting dark and we figured we were going to have to find another bridge to sleep under when a car passed us then put on its brakes and pulled over. When we ran up to the car and were shocked to see a young couple with a small baby inside. I was sure they were stopping for some reason other than picking us up, but to my amazement they asked where we were going. When we told them Florida the woman said that, "It must be your lucky day because we are going to Pensacola." While I certainly wanted the ride I couldn't help but tell them that we were in pretty rough shape and hadn't showered in days, so if they didn't want us to ride with them and their child I certainly would understand. The lady said they were Christians and we didn't look like murderers as she invited us to get in the car. That wonderful young family not only stopped at a truck stop where Jerry and I could take a shower, but also bought us something to eat.

We hitched a ride from Pensacola to Tampa, where I was hoping to find my brother Jack. I had his address in my wallet and sure enough he was home when we arrived. Jack was very happy to see me and we spent most of the week reminiscing about old times, especially those times when he would skip work, I would skip school, and we would go fishing. If I had known that the week I stayed with him would be the last time I would spend any quality time with him except for one the day in 1975, two weeks before he was killed, I would have stayed longer and told him how much I loved him.

After the week in Tampa I decided it was time to roll on back to New York. Jack gave me a present, the car a guy had given him to hold as collateral for a personal loan. Jack said that the guy was late in paying him back so he filled the gas tank and sent Jerry and me on our way in it. We made it to South Carolina before running out of gas. Jerry suggested that we cut a piece of garden hose to siphon gas from parked cars and continue driving to New York.

It was tempting however, I decided to sell the car to a junk dealer at a salvage yard. I knew Jack would tell the owner that car had been stolen. Considering the plates and registration were in the owner's name, I knew it would be better to dump it at a scrap yard for a few bucks than risk being caught and face grand larceny charges. The scrap dealer realized we were dumping the car and that it was most likely stolen, so only offered me forty bucks for it, no questions asked. I took the forty bucks and away we went straight to a restaurant. After ravenously chowing down on hamburgers, hot dogs, and milk shakes we were back to hitchhiking again.

We hitched our way into North Carolina where we ended up stranded in a cold wind-driven rainstorm at midnight. As we walked along hoping to find a bridge to seek shelter under along came a bus. We flagged the bus down frantically waiving our arms so the driver would see us. I anticipated using the remaining money to buy tickets to the next bus station, dry out, and wait for the weather to break before continuing our trek north. The bus ground to a halt and as soon as the door opened we rushed up the steps with a sigh of relief.

As I asked the driver how much it would cost to the next station, I glanced down the isle only to see that the bus was empty. Quickly looking back at the driver I realized he was wearing soiled overalls. He told us that he had completed repairs on the bus and was headed to his home for the night before taking it to Raleigh to be put back in service in the morning. Seeing our hearts sink and the pathetic condition we were in, the driver allowed us to sleep on the bus and ride with him to Raleigh in the morning.

When we arrived at his home not only did he bring out blankets for us, but also gave us hot coffee and sandwiches. Then to our amazement he left the bus running with the heaters on all night! In the morning his wife sent out a breakfast of eggs, sausage, toast, and grits. All the calloused hardness of my tormented soul was challenged by that amazing bus mechanic and his wife's grace and mercy. I have no doubt that it was Grandma's intercessory prayers; begging God to protect and bring her wayward grandson home safely, that destined the wonderful Christian couple in Alabama and the bus mechanic in North Carolina to cross my path.

When Jerry and I finally arrived in New York a series of events unfolded. First, within three weeks Jerry vanished and I never saw him again. Second, I couldn't get the indelible picture of what happened in Alabama and North Carolina out of my mind. Third, after reuniting with our chapter of the KingsMen I was told that the club house in Lockport had been raided again and was now closed. Fourth, when we were drinking with Chuck and Jim, two members of the North Tonawanda Chapter of the KingsMen, the subject of narcotics agents came up. As we discussed drug deals, Chuck pointed out a young guy at the bar who he thought was an informant. I didn't believe the dorky looking guy was anything more than a punk who wanted to hang around the bar to be near the gang.

They told us they were going to kill the guy because he was a "rat." I guess they meant it because a week later the guy's body washed up on the beach along Lake Ontario sporting a crushed skull and two cement blocks tied to it. Upon investigation, the Police found that Chuck and Jim had left the bar with the guy and one of their relatives, a teenage girl. They drove to the shore of Lake Ontario where they bludgeoned him to death while the girl witnessed the entire act. How stupid! The girl gave the Police a blow by blow description of the act resulting in more than enough evidence for a conviction.

Off they went to join Tommy at Attica with 25-years-to-life sentences. I could go on for a quite a few more pages however, I believe you get the picture by now and I am being spiritually attacked just recounting those very dark demonic times. Get behind me Satan-I am washed in the blood of the Lamb.

As the consequences of the vile emptiness, constant degradation, and perversion of the gang life tormented my soul, you might think I would succumb to Grandma's prayers and come out of the darkness. Not me, come to the mercy of Christ? No, instead I left the gang and joined a group of hippies living in a commune in Zoar Valley near Gowanda, NY.

When I joined the hippie commune the draw wasn't peace, love, and tranquility, or even the abundance of illegal drugs. The draw was free love, free sex, and the large pool of young women who ascribed to that philosophy. An added bonus of living in the hippie commune was that it wasn't hard to pick the girls you wanted to enjoy this sexual revolution with, because everyone ran around naked.

I found out rather quickly that the utopian society concept of altruistic sharing of the land and everything else while we all lived together in perfect harmony was merely a fantasy and an illusion. In reality, the same social hierarchy existed in the hippie commune as in the traditional society. Leaders evolved in much the same fashion using a strong personality, manipulation, and at last resort Bullying others into submission I became a leader within a very short time resulting in my having the pick of the litter.

If you were to belong to a hippie community, how do you think "your family" would procure basic needs like food, water, beer, drugs, female hygiene products, and vehicles to transport you to concerts with no income? There were three basic ways: first, getting money from our families and friends back in the "straight, hypocritical society" we were escaping; second by stealing them, which we became very proficient at; and third, by becoming entrepreneurs, selling drugs and at times our women.

On occasions I would drive my 1960 Dodge Lancer hippie-mobile back home to visit Mom, Gram, and a few other friends to hit them up for money. I would buy food, beer and drugs, usually marijuana and psychotropic pills, then head back to the Valley. I always returned to the valley using the back roads because the hippie-mobile was uninsured and had expired registration and plates. Other commune members would do the same thing, especially the girls.

When we traveled to rock concerts we sold drugs to pay for our expenses. We would go to local drug stores and buy gelatin capsules which we emptied and refilled with drugs. Of course we also cut them with sugar, baking soda, or other fillers to make them go farther and be more profitable. Sometimes we just filled them with baking soda, selling them during the concert so by the time buyers realized they had been ripped off, we were long gone. Contrary to a common myth, there is no honor among thieves.

Standard accommodations in a hippie commune are tents pitched in the woods, a lifestyle that brings a few discomforts with it. First, crabs; everyone was plagued with them so Blue Ointment was at the top of our *rip-off from the pharmacy list*. Another annoyance was lice which weren't as prevalent as crabs, but if you were infected, the itching and scratching were a hellish nightmare.

However, the worst plague every commune encountered was the passing of sexually transmitted diseases (STD) which often was at epidemic proportions. The problem was always exacerbated when we shared or sold our women at the concerts. They would pick up the prevalent diseases of that local area. Consequently, every time we followed the rock concerts into a new city we would find the free medical clinics to get antibiotics, usually tetracycline which was used to cure a myriad of venereal diseases.

While most of the sexually transmitted diseases were easily cured by antibiotics, occasionally someone would contract a virulent strain of syphilis landing them in the hospital. One of the girls in our commune was raped by a KingsMen when a group from the Olean Chapter came to Zoar Valley to party. I knew the guy, who was nicknamed Moose, and remembered he had contracted a drug resistant STD from a girl in Olean a year earlier when I was still in the gang. Sure enough our girl became infected.

The biggest threat in the valley, however, wasn't the KingsMen, sexually transmitted diseases, crabs or lice; the biggest threat in the valley was undercover narcotics agents. Because of the volume of illegal drugs used and sold in the Valley, it was a prime target of the undercover narcotics agents. Sale of drugs in New York State under the Rockefeller drug laws was punishable by a sentence of one day to life in prison. That meant that if you were convicted of selling a joint to an undercover cop you could spend the rest of your life in Attica Prison.

Thankfully, we recognized a number of the narcotics agents because they had busted so many of our friends. And for additional security I always had my German Sheppard named Bo with me. Bo was as mean as a rattlesnake even biting me at least once a day. If some one came up to my car Bo would go nuts trying to attack them through the window. Not once did a police officer ever ask me to step out of my car when they stopped me because Bo was so intimidating. The police officer had to decide if the stop was worth being attacked and discretion was always the better choice.

I seldom drove my car over the speed limit or broke any other vehicle and traffic laws so I seldom was pulled over. Those rare times I was stopped, however, Bo was my savior. Another tactic we used as a precaution was to have under age kids sell the drugs for us. They could not be prosecuted if they were arrested; only sent to family court. However, we clearly understood there was always the risk of being busted for possession or sale of drugs. I learned that firsthand when I came into the valley one Saturday afternoon with a load of marijuana only to recognize an undercover agent dressed as a hippie asking a group of teenagers where he could buy the best drugs in the valley. I shuddered as I heard them say, "See Alex, he has the best drugs." *See Alex? See you later!*

Bo and I bailed out of the valley and as I drove onto the bridge which crossed over the Cattaraugus Creek in Gowanda, I threw all the drugs over the side and hightailed it as fast and as far from Zoar Valley as I could get. I had enough Marijuana to receive about 3,000 years in Attica Prison and I knew Attica wasn't a nice place to spend the rest of your life in because some of my friends were already there.

I decided it was time to go back home and give up the hippie life, all those drugs, and stick to good old legal beer to get high. I was totally burnt out on the whole scene anyway, the KingsMen, hippies, drugs, diseases, and critters; I had experienced more than enough! I actually pulled my car over and thanked God for listening to the prayers of my righteous, constantly praying Grandmother. I figured that the only logical reason I had never been arrested or killed was because Grandma had a direct line to Jesus, and constantly pleaded for my mercy and protection-and of course she was! When I returned home Mom, Gram, and our extended family were ecstatic, I was finally ending my pilgrimage through Hell.

I wasn't sure what I was going to do but I did know that it had been a long, long road that led me back home.

CHAPTER 14

PLAYING TO WIN

—m—

The first few weeks at home all I did was soak in a hot bath, sleep in a soft bed, devour Gram's great cooking, chill out, and let my drug and alcohol saturated mind clear out. When I was finally rested and rejuvenated, I resumed the only thing I was very good at, drinking and fighting. I went back to my old hangout the Val Hal La Bar in Corfu and started tending bar there. If I wasn't working or drinking at the Val Hal La I would frequent other bars hustling money by playing pool or cards while hustling girls for sex. I had a long list of girls I charmed out of their pants and into my bed.

I ran into a problem with these girls because they weren't commune or gang girls who you had sex with, thanked, and went on to the next one. Instead, these girls became attached and possessive. When they became pregnant they didn't want to run to Buffalo for a quickie abortion they wanted me to keep the child, accept responsibility, and get married! Yikes responsibility, marriage, NOT! Get an abortion or get down the road. Some did eventually get abortions while some put the child up for adoption and some kept their babies.

One girl brought the baby to Mom's house trying to enlist her support in an effort to convince me to marry her.

That baby, now a young man, wrote me a letter saying that his mother told him I was his father. He went on to say that his aunt had told him that I was a great man, and a judge. I was able to tell him that I wasn't a great man and begged his forgiveness for the pain he had suffered because of me.

I have been forgiven for the terrible pain, suffering, and death I caused, however, I live with the reality that at any time there might be someone at my door who I fathered. I praise God for the ones that are alive but still mourn over the innocent blood I spilled. As I have said before abortion, regardless of the agenda driven spin it gets, is also a man's issue.

A friend of mine, Joe Leto who owned the Val Hal La Bar, and I would often go bar hopping to the many other saloons thriving in the area. One of them, the Log Cabin Bar, was a beautiful, rustic log building perched at the edge of a falls overlooking Tonawanda Creek in Indian Falls. It had been recently purchased by a family from Buffalo. The owners, Ed and Evelyn DuPont, sold their home in Buffalo using the proceeds to purchase the business which had been Ed's life long dream.

The only problem was that Ed was a poor businessman and drove most patrons away leaving a select few who barely bought enough beer to pay the bills. Additionally, he kept two vicious German Shepherds behind the bar. If anyone put a hand over the bar the dogs would attempt to attack them which also drove customers away.

Ed and his wife, Evelyn, fought like cats and dogs. Evelyn attacked anything and everything Ed said and belittled him unmercifully. When the war became unbearable Ed would nod to me as his eyes glanced toward the door which was his sign for me to get the car ready and away we would go bar hopping in Akron or to his old watering holes in Buffalo. Ed's life revolved around drinking so he knew everyone in every bar we drank at.

He would brag about how his son Edward Jr. received a full scholarship to Rutgers University to play football. He always left out the fact that Ed Junior was expelled because of academic failure the first semester and then joined the Marines which he was being discharged from for bad behavior. Ed bragged that his son was going to be a Deputy Sheriff when he came home from the Marines. I remember thinking, if Junior couldn't hack it in college and was being thrown out of the Marines while in basic training, he surely wouldn't be hired as a Deputy Sheriff.

However, if Ed needed believe that his son was going to be a Deputy Sheriff it was okay with me. After all the poor guy was being neutered by his wicked witch of a wife every day, at least I could cut him a little slack. What I quickly realized when I met Ed Jr. was that he was the apple of Evelyn's eye and could do no wrong. If Ed wanted a motorcycle, Mom bought him a new Harley Davidson Sportster. If Ed needed, money out of the cash register it came. What ever Eddie wanted Eddie got.

What was also more than obvious was that Eddie was the only family member that received love and favor from Evelyn. Her oldest daughter Sandy, second oldest daughter Kathy, and the youngest Geraldine, who everyone called Gerry Ellen, were left to grovel for crumbs of attention, with none of the girls receiving positive reinforcement much less unconditional love.

Gerry Ellen wasn't even taken to the doctor when she was terribly sick with a blood infection which she almost died from! Why? Because it cost too much to see a doctor. Only Eddie could go to a private Catholic School, Gerry Ellen had to attend public school! Why? Because it was too expensive to send her to private school. Gerry couldn't go to the dentist to have her two eye teeth which protruded out like fangs removed! Why? You guessed it, the cost was prohibitive.

However, Eddie, who the sun rose and set on could have anything he wanted, he was Momma's golden boy.

Gerry Ellen seldom smiled and was extremely withdrawn because she was so embarrassed. First of all, if she smiled everyone would see her humiliating eye teeth, second, and even more heart wrenching, she had been emotionally crushed by her mother since birth. Gerry Ellen could not please her Mother in any way no matter how hard she tried. She received 100's on English tests at school yet that wasn't good enough! Now tell me how do you do better than perfect?

The saddest and most devastating part of Gerry Ellen's life was that her Mother demanded perfection and withheld her love unless she performed flawlessly. Yet even when she performed without a flaw, Evelyn still never accepted the perfection she demanded. Evelyn never said the words "I love you," to Gerry Ellen, however, made sure she knew that she her never wanted another child after Eddie was born, and that Gerry was a mistake. What a wonderful, nurturing way to treat your daughter, it would definitely make her feel loved, accepted, and secure wouldn't it?

And while it was bad enough that acceptance was conditional, the collateral conditions to receive it were unattainable. As a result, Gerry Ellen was systematically programmed to believe that if she ever broke the rules established by her Ayatollah Mother or anyone in authority, the consequences would be so severe she might not survive.

She was also warned that if she violated the laws, values, and standards, her punishment would be severe. She literally didn't dare establish her own personal identity or risk being anything other than what her mother defined her as: an unwanted child that was a burden and unable to give or receive love. What I didn't realize was that Gerry Ellen saw in me a handsome free spirited hunk of manhood which epitomized the freedom and identity she longed for.

One night in January 1971, Ed Senior went outside of the bar to get wood for the fireplace and dropped dead. Evelyn decided to keep the casket closed. Even in death she still took one last jab at him scornfully commenting, "Now look what he has gone and done." I guess he wasn't supposed to die without her permission. For poor Gerry Ellen, the only person who gave her any semblance of unconditional love was gone. Sadly, for many years after her father's death she struggled with not being able to gain closure by seeing his body in the casket. She just wasn't able to accept the reality that her Dad was dead.

With Ed gone, a dwindling clientele, and the bill collector at the door, Evelyn contemplated closing the bar. Because I was one of the few regular customers still frequenting the place, Evelyn asked me what she could do to try to save the business and make the bar profitable. She knew I bartended at the Blue Inn and Val Hal La, and was very good at the bar business; therefore might be able to help make hers profitable. She was right, if there was anything I was good at it was sin and the bar business. I asked her to give me $100 which she hesitantly retrieved from the cash register and handed it to me asking why I wanted it. I told her that she would just have to trust me.

Taking the $100, I told her to watch the bar, which wasn't hard to do with the only other patrons in the place being Buck and Hattie Sliker who lived just a stone's throw up the road. I served Buck and Hattie a couple of free beers and asked them to keep Ma, as we now called Evelyn, company until I returned. Within an hour I was back responding to the puzzled look on Ma's face by again assuring her to, "Just trust me."

Because I didn't want to drive the 18 miles all the way back to Moms and Gram's house I slept on a shelf in the kitchen of the bar. The next night, which was a Saturday night I asked Ma for another $100. She looked at me with an askance stare to which I again replied that she would have to trust me. She grumbled something under her breath to the effect that, "This is the last hundred you'll get out of me," as she reluctantly handed me the money. I immediately left the bar telling Ma I would be right back. I think she believed I was scamming her and about to go AWOL after beating her out of two hundred bucks. In an hour I was back at the bar which seemed to be a little reassuring to her. She asked what I had done with the money since she couldn't really afford to give anything much less $200. I told her to just wait and see.

Within an hour the bar was loaded with people drinking and having a good time. Ma was astonished and shook her head as she asked how I got all those people to come to the bar. I explained that with the first $100 she gave me I went to the Val Hal La, the Gables bar, and the bars at both bowling alleys in Corfu buying a few rounds of drinks.

At each place I told everyone that I was now the manager of the Log Cabin Bar, inviting them to stop down and see us. I took the second $100 and returned to the same bars buying a couple more rounds and again invited everyone to stop down and see us. My buddy, Joe Leto, the owner of the Val Hal La even closed his bar early that Saturday night to come down and party with us.

As I said before, I knew how to do sin extremely well. With in two months we were having pool tournaments complete with 50-cent draft beer and a free buffet for everyone. The first Saturday of the month, the top six players with the highest scores on the shuffle board bowling machine played a one game championship with the winner receiving a twelve gauge Ithaca Deer Slayer shotgun. It cost a quarter to play each game with a maximum of six players. There were people playing that bowling machine from the time we opened until we closed, all with a vision of winning that beautiful shot gun. We had to empty the machines quarter bin at least twice daily because it would be completely full.

Every afternoon we catered to the working men with happy hour selling half-priced drinks from four to six p.m. On Friday nights we accommodated the young and the restless with a total party attitude including blaring rock and roll music and draft beer with the night usually ending in a good fashioned old brawl or two. Our Saturday afternoon pool tournaments, free buffet, and the bowling machine humming became the staple of the local beer drinking community. With business booming and the place always packed, our profits poured in faster than we could pour draft beer.

After the pool and bowling machine crowd staggered home usually at about five o'clock, we quickly swept and mopped the bar getting ready for the senior citizen crowd who came to dance to the live piano and organ music. The senior citizens were our best customers; they drank the more expensive mixed drinks and always ordered roast beef or steak sandwiches. They came early, danced until it was late, and never wrecked the joint.

Another money making bonanza was selling six packs and cases of beer to the campers from Indian Falls Lake Camp Grounds located just up the road from us. When they ran out of beer and all the stores were closed they came to us more than willing to pay our highly inflated prices, usually twice the normal cost for the beer. That great American institution, supply and demand, resulted in windfall profits for the bar. Within one year we made so much money our book keeper couldn't hide it anymore. We applied for and were granted a building permit to double the size of the place.

Everything was going just great with money pouring in and Ed Jr. and I becoming closer than brothers. The bar also provided an inexhaustible pool of party girls and sex partners. However, I did notice that Gerry Ellen appeared to become jealous over the girls and it seemed that she had a crush on me. However, because she was so introverted and quiet I just wasn't sure besides I was like a big brother, nine years older than her. I did flirt with Gerry Ellen because it was the only time I could get her to smile.

The bar was more than a full time job leading Ed, Ma, and me to all live there. Ma slept on the pool table while Ed and I slept in the kitchen, Ed on the floor and me on a bench like counter top. We also had their two white German Shepherd sleeping with us along with a raccoon we named Rocky. One of the Indian customers gave Rocky to us when he was a baby and we nurtured him until he matured.

It was an amazing site to see our whole crew sleeping in that bar, Ma snoring away on the pool table, Ed and one of the dogs on the floor, and the other dog next to me on the counter, with Rocky curled up sleeping on the side of the dog.

Having a full grown raccoon living with you in a bar sometimes created a few wild situations. When we opened the pool table to remove the quarter bin we often put Rocky inside of it. Rocky loved to scurry around the inside of the table and chase the pool balls as they rolled down from the pockets. Unsuspecting people would be playing a game of pool when Rocky would reach his little furry paw up through the pockets of the table and grab a pool ball pulling it down into the hole. The players would freak out claiming that something had just reached up through the hole grabbing their pool ball.

Of course everyone who knew Rocky was in the table would act like the stunned players were crazy asking if they had two much to drink and were "seeing things." Then all of a sudden this furry paw would come up through the pocket again feeling around for another ball. If there was no ball near the hole down his little paw would disappear only to come up through another hole as the players screamed, "There it is again!" it was hilarious.

Rocky not only enjoyed grabbing balls off the pool table he also loved to walk along the bar and under the bar stools looking for tidbits of pretzels, popcorn, peanuts, along with other choice morsels patrons dropped on the floor. However, we ran into a small problem one afternoon while Rocky made his rounds under the bar stools. One of our patrons, Peggy, a lady who loved to wear skirts that at best only came to mid-thigh, was eating peanuts. As I served her a draft beer I came eye to eye with Peg instantly realizing she was in extreme distress by the horrific look on her wide-eyed face.

Before I could ask her what her problem was she jumped off the bar stool screeching at the top of her lungs in panic as she hurriedly waddled toward the exit door. I immediately recognized her dilemma; there were Rocky's back legs and tail hanging down below her skirt between her legs! By the time she and Rocky got out the door everyone in the bar was roaring. After wiping my tears of laughter away on a bar cloth, I went to rescue Rocky. As I opened the door there he was coming up the stairs with Peg's pink underwear over his head. Peg was no where to be found.

Every day we let Rocky out for his daily hour or two romps around the outside of the bar and along the creek. However, one day we didn't hear his normal scratching at the door, his signal that he wanted to come back in. We looked for him for weeks all to no avail; he was gone. Finally we were forced to conclude that he wanted to be free. It wasn't long before we found out two things, first, Rocky wasn't a boy, and second *she* had brought her brood of baby raccoons back home with her.

A few months later she took off with her family only to return alone with a rear end full of shot gun pellets. Ma nursed her back to health then away she went this time never to return. Everyone missed Mrs. Rocky well everyone except Peg. We often reminisced about her escapades including, bringing her babies home, Peg's underwear caper, the times she would knock over the whiskey bottles licking up the spills and ending up staggering around the bar in a drunken stupor and coming home to have Ma nurse her back to health.

CHAPTER 15

BROKEN IS AS BROKEN DOES

—ᚾᚾᚲ—

B ecause our bar was located less than two miles from the Tonawanda Indian Reservation many Indians frequented it. Some local establishments didn't cater to them discouraging Native Americans from coming to their bars.

However, we welcomed the Indians, sponsoring a bowling team called the Log Cabin Indians comprised of four Indian men and me. We were so good that we won the League championship. We also sponsored a softball team, again, called The Log Cabin Indians which was again, all Indians except for me. We challenged other bars' softball teams to beer games with the losing team having to pay for a keg of beer. When we played the stands were filled with people from the reservation cheering for "their team," and of course many came to our bar after the game to help drink the beer.

One of my best friends from the reservation, Sanford Jonathon known as "Dude," brought his family to our bar almost every day. One of his children, an eight year old boy named Sidney, could out drink many adults. I drank with Dude and Sidney on many occasions and everyone thought it very funny to see Sidney passed out along side of Dude and me in the back of my van. Dude and I were "Blood

Brothers," having performed the traditional Indian ritual of cutting of our palms with a knife and grasping hands, "mixing our blood" which signified that we were brothers forever. In a break with conventional wisdom, we allowed Dude to run up a bar bill, something we seldom permitted anyone to do.

Dude and Bonnie drank everyday, usually running the bill up very high. He would pay for part of the bill when he worked which was spotty at best. His tab grew so high that Dude gave us one of his horses, "Miss White," as payment. He also had a horse named "Spook" that was extremely high strung, ran very fast, and at times went where ever he felt like going no matter how the rider tried to control him.

One day Dude rode Spook to the bar. I asked him if I could take Gerry Ellen for a ride down by the creek and back. Gerry Ellen was a little hesitant but because she had a crush on me, agreed to go. Everything was going just fine until Spook decided to return to the bar at full gallop. He abruptly stopped, unceremoniously launching Gerry Ellen over the top of me. She still has gravel in her wrist from that swan dive into our parking lot. I guess it was love at first scar, and if she knew how many more scars I would cause her she might have run away from both the horse and me.

The Indians loved to have parties most of which lasted all weekend long. They would set up very large tents and start a bash on Friday night that went full tilt boogie until Sunday afternoon. One Saturday night, actually Sunday morning after we closed the bar, Ed and I went over to the reservation to join one of the parties. The tent was full of people, mostly Indians having a great time drinking, dancing, and telling funny stories. It was fairly light out this particular night because of a full moon. After we partied for about a half-hour, I asked Dude if I could take Spook for a ride and of course he said I could. However, he informed me that because someone borrowed his bridle and saddle, I would have to ride bareback and steer Spook by pushing my hand on the side of his neck to make him turn.

I walked the 100 yards to Dude's house, hopped on Spook's back, and away we went. Putting my hand on his neck to steer him toward the tent, sure enough he decided that was exactly where he wanted to go. As we approached the party at full gallop, I futilely tried to get Spook to stop. While he slowed down a little, he decided that we needed to say hello to everyone in the tent. Flying through the festivities, I heard people screaming, beer and whisky bottles crashing, and the record player smashing. And as we exited the other side of the tent, people were yelling, "Get that crazy white man off that horse!" While I agreed with their assessment of the situation, Spook didn't! About that time he decided one trip through the revelry just wasn't enough and headed right back through it again. After I secured Spook back at his pasture, I immediately headed back to our bar to retrieve a peace offering: a keg of beer and a half-dozen bottles of whiskey, all was forgiven.

By now Ed and I were closer than natural brothers. We worked the bar six days a week and when we had time off, would head to Buffalo to party. Many of Ed's old friends owned or worked at the wildest bars in the city, such as Mr. Good Bar and Aliota'a Club. Aliota's Club featured bands and in fact the Allman Brothers band played there in their early days.

Mr. Good Bar was one of our favorite haunts because it was loaded with girls from Buffalo State College and because Ed was close friends with the owners, manager, and most of the bartenders. We seldom if ever had to pay for a drink and even better were invited to the owner's apartment above the bar for the wildest parties full of sex, drugs, and rock and roll. The apartment always had large bowls full of Cocaine, THC, and the devil only knew what other drugs waiting, with straws lined up all around them.

There were also plentiful amounts of Marijuana and Hashish to be smoked. Ed and I would get so wasted we couldn't drive home until the next day. Mark, one of the bartenders at Mr. Good Bar, would also invite us to his apartment across from the University of Buffalo for great parties. One night after Mr. Good Bar closed, we went to Mark's apartment to party. He told us that he had some dynamite drugs he wanted us to try. He had the same set up, a large bowl with straws all around.

Ed and I sat down beside the bowl and snorted a large amount of the powder, wham, it knocked me flat. At the same time, I heard Ed hit the floor and moan, "Wow." In an instant I was so high I thought I was going to nod out and felt nauseous like when overdosing on pain killers or heroin. When I was finally able to get enough control to say anything audible, I called out "ACE," which was my nickname for Ed, only to have him half-whisper, "I can't move."

We lay on that floor for over three hours before we started to come down enough to talk. We would say a few words then bounce back into a stupor and nod out for another five or ten minutes. After an hour of drifting in and out of stupors we gained enough control to drive back out to the Cabin. As we drove away from Mark's apartment a Buffalo Police car immediately pulled right along side of us. Both cops stared intently at us causing Ed to become paranoid. He was still feeling the residual affects of the drugs and asked me if he was driving okay. I was still so high I couldn't tell but replied, "You must be because the cops are pulling away." We realized why the police were so interested in us when Mark's apartment was raided by the Buffalo Narcotics Squad the next night. I guess he couldn't stand the thought of being incarcerated at Attica for the rest of his life; he hung himself.

Ed and I kept going to Buffalo to party, however, we seldom stayed overnight because everyone was paranoid of drug busts after Mark's fate. One Saturday night I talked Ed into making a trip to Zoar Valley on his motorcycle to party with my old hippie friends. We stopped in Eden at Roellers Hotel which Aunt Gerry and Uncle Howard sold after their retirement.

It was nostalgic being there as I showed Eddie all around the place. We had a few drinks then with our remaining money bought a case of beer to take to the valley. As we left the bar with the case of beer resting between us, some local guys from the bar yelled insults at us. Eddie responded with a hearty "F_ _ _ You!" and the chase began. As they came up behind us Ed threw a beer bottle which crashed on their windshield prompting them to cut us off.

Before they could get out of their car I flew off the bike and struck the driver in the head with a beer bottle as Ed began fighting with the other guys getting out of the car. It was raining fairly hard by then and we rolled around fighting in the road for awhile. The scene was rather comical with everyone rolling around in pitch darkness not knowing who they were hitting. When it was all said and done we ended up shaking hands and laughingly declared it a draw.

At that point we should have turned around and headed back home to the Cabin; we were soaking wet and covered with mud. However, we decided it was closer to go to the valley and into a tent than ride the 30-miles back home. I was driving the bike as we entered Zoar Valley where we had to go down a very steep path that was not easy to negotiate on a dry sunny day. Ed tapped me on the shoulder asking if I wanted to stop and walk the bike down to the bottom to which I replied, "No problem just hang on," as I started down the path.

We went about ten feet when the front tire caught in a rut causing the bike to veer left and over the side of the embankment. All I could feel as I flew over the handle bars into midair was the beer bottles hitting my back. I tumbled over and over for what seemed an eternity until I felt a sudden jolt and everything went blank.

I had slammed into a tree with the back of the motorcycle helmet hitting first. The next thing I remember I was lying in a heap hearing Ed's muffled call, "Alex, Alex, where are you?" After I cleared most of the mud and blood out of my mouth I called back, "Ace I'm down here."

I began climbing up the steep mud covered incline but kept sliding back down. When I finally reached the top Ed and I pulled the bike from the tree it had caught on just as I went over the handlebars. Ed had pushed himself off the back of the bike as we began to veer off the path, and was fine. As we were pulling the bike up on to the path I felt a beer bottle on the ground. It wasn't broken so I opened it to get a drink and wash out the remainder of mud, blood, and stones from my mouth. Ed grabbed it and deposited it over the side of the hill, complaining that I had wrecked his motorcycle and all I could think of was having a beer.

We sat down and had a good laugh, then nursed the bike down the path and finally arrived at the hippie camp. After all we endured; there was no one there to party with. The next morning it was still raining and to make maters worse it was much colder with the temperature only about 45-degrees. After assessing the damage to the bike, which was minimal, we limped our way back toward home. As we approached Buffalo the cold rain had turned to sleet and we were freezing. We stopped at a Mexican restaurant and asked what we could buy with the 96-cents we had between us. The guy behind the counter pointed to the hot peppers. We split four hot peppers desperately hoping they would warm us up. And while they burned our mouths, they did little for the rest our body, and we froze all the way home.

God works in strange ways His wonders to perform. One morning after returning from an all night party in Buffalo, Ed and I sat on the rocks overlooking the waterfalls by the bar smoking marijuana and listening to a tape of the Allman Brothers Band. As I sat there mellow and melancholy watching the gorgeous sunrise I was overpowered with a feeling to share the Gospel of Jesus Christ with Eddie.

Ed was raised Catholic, went to Catholic Schools, and knew nothing about being born again. He was actually a bad Catholic never attending church, but staunch in his Catholic beliefs even though he couldn't explain what they were. I went through the biblical concept of being born again, explaining what it meant to be saved. I couldn't help but think that here I was acting just like Grandma when she shared the Lord with the motorcycle gang.

Ed looked at me as if I was crazy retorting that the Protestant Bible may say you had to be born again but the Catholic Bible didn't. I asked if he ever read or studied his Catholic Bible to which he replied, "No." Ed rolled another joint and as he passed it to me, declared the discussion about Jesus was over.

The bar business was great, things were hopping and we were extremely busy. Ed, Ma, Gerry Ellen, and I were spending a lot of time there which also meant Gerry Ellen and I were spending a lot of time together. It wasn't long until I was taking advantage of her infatuation with me and having sex with her. I had at least two other girls pregnant at the time and trying to juggle the mess was not very easy. One girl's father even came to the Cabin to try and intimidate me into marrying his pregnant daughter with threats of physical harm. The tactic backfired when I challenged him, his family, or anyone he sent to try and harm me, guaranteeing that whoever tried wouldn't be going back home, but instead to the hospital or the grave. The sad reality is that this wasn't just an idle threat, I meant it.

When Ed decided that we should run the bar as a total party bar I was shocked and dismayed. All the time and effort I had put in to make the place a goldmine was all going to be thrown away. I relied on Ma who would I knew never give up the goldmine and her future to turn the place into a party bar. Ed told me that he was going to force her out of the bar and take over.

How he accomplished getting Ma to leave haunts me to this day and I am sure it also haunts Ed. On the next Saturday night after we closed the bar, I was in my bed on the kitchen counter and heard an altercation between Ed and Ma in the barroom. About the time Ma told Ed that he couldn't ruin the business by turning it into a party bar, I suddenly heard a loud crack followed by a scream of pain and a thud. Ed had punched Ma in the face breaking her glasses and knocking her to the floor. I was astounded, I had hurt a lot of people in fights however, I couldn't imagine ever punching my mother any other mother in the face. I heard Ma crying as she left the bar and drove away.

Gerry Ellen and I stayed at the bar for a few months then left for two reasons. First, I couldn't get the terrible picture of Ed punching his mother in the face out of my mind. Second, Ed and his new girl friend Shelly BlueEye, an Indian girl I knew all to well from my days with the Akron KingsMen, couldn't get along with Gerry Ellen and me. It was sad to see what I had worked so hard to develop into what I knew would be a business that would easily support Ma, Ed, Gerry Ellen, and I, being wrecked. Sure enough with in a year Ed dropped the keys off to Ma along with all the unpaid bills telling her that he and Shelly, who he had since married, were done with the Cabin and just walked away.

Ma asked me if I wanted to try to resurrect the business and save the bar. However, things had changed significantly during that year. Gerry Ellen was pregnant, and when I took her to Buffalo to have an abortion, God stepped in. Because she was so terrified of having to tell Ma and the rest of the family that she was pregnant, she agreed to have the abortion. I took her to the Tudor Lounge where I had taken other girls to arrange abortions however, something hit my soul as I looked back at Gerry Ellen sitting in the corner of that bar looking totally scared and helpless.

I left the bar to finalize the deal for her abortion but when I came back she told me that she couldn't "murder this baby." I replied, "Okay, I'll marry you." We now have been married for 36 years. That baby she wouldn't murder, Robert E. Alexander II, is a school teacher whose wife, also a teacher, brought Robert E. Alexander III into this world five years ago. Through sobs and a river of tears I praise God for his mercy.

I wish I could end this story now with a chapter telling how 36 years ago on July 29th 1972, I married Gerry Ellen, we both got saved and everything has been wonderful ever since. Like I said I would like to, but it is now that the story really begins.

CHAPTER 16

FALLING FORWARD

—〰—

Here I was married with a pregnant wife and in desperate need of a job. As I searched the "Help Wanted" section in the newspaper, I realized finding a good job to support my soon to be family was not going to be an easy task. There were no companies advertising for an experienced: former motorcycle gang member and/or ex-hippie to raise havoc and destruction, sell drugs, and abuse women.

I worked menial jobs as a laborer for a paving company, a helper on a roofing crew, and for the Department of Conservation. Now the conservation position was a challenging and fun job even if tagging deer and wild geese only paid minimum wage. Oh, by the way, if you ever get a job as a laborer there, don't listen to any of the Conservation Officers if they tell you wild Geese are tame and lovable. And whatever you do, *don't ever stick your tongue out at one of those "tame, loveable geese"* when you are placing an identification tag on its leg.

The Conservation Officer talked me into doing just that. About the time I stuck my tongue half-way out that darn goose latched onto it and tried to yank it out of my mouth. Did you know that goose bills are full of small extremely sharp teeth, well I sure do. By the time I strangled that goose long enough to get it to release my tongue the entire crew were laughing their fool heads off. My tongue was sore for weeks.

I exacted my revenge on the Conservation Officer a few weeks later when I was told to take a tractor equipped with a brush cutter and mow the banks of the feeding ponds. Everything was going along smoothly until I came over an embankment where I hit a wood Chuck hole. The tractor's front end bounced high in the air and when it came down; there I was heading right into a pond.

Before I could hit the brakes I was sitting in the middle of the pond with water up to my chest. The only part of the tractor sticking out was approximately six inches of its exhaust pipe. I got off the sunken tractor, walked back to our locker room, changed my clothes, and then told the Head Conservation Officer, named Ollie, that I got the tractor stuck back by the third pond. He told one of the other workers to take our dump truck to pull my tractor out. I told him that we needed our D8 bull dozer to accomplish the task. Ollie scoffed replying that we didn't need any D8 bulldozer because our dump truck could pull the tractor out of any mud hole I could get it stuck in. He condescendingly told me to jump in the truck and he would show this rookie how strong the truck was.

Every one went back to the pond to see Ollie make a fool out of me again. As we crested the embankment of the third pond Ollie said "Where is the tractor, are we at the wrong pond?" I assured him that we were indeed at the right pond. Ollie tilted his head and made his face contort into a gesture that suggested I was crazy. I told him to look very closely at the middle of the pond as I pointed to the six inches of exhaust pipe sticking above of the water. Ollie, in stoic fashion, squinted at the pond and said, "Maybe your right kid, Jimmy go back and get the dozer." By that time everyone on the crew was laughing and asking Ollie if he was going to swim out and hook the chain to the tractor. Ollie looked at me with a smile and said, "We're even kid."

Joe Leto, who owned the Val Hal La bar in Corfu, also owned the Pizzeria in Oakfield, NY. He told me that I could remodel the upstairs rooms and rent them to use as an apartment for Gerry Ellen and our soon-to-be family. I painted the ceilings, installed paneling on the walls and tile on the floors.

Our's was not your typical bathroom. The toilet sat at the end of a ten-foot long by thirty-six-inch wide room, and was hooked up to a hot water line. When you flushed, steam rose out of the toilet. Having hot water in the toilet had its benefits especially during cold weather. Because there was little or no heat in the bathroom flushing the toilet two or three times helped make the room and your buns warm.

There we were a happy family, Gerry Ellen who was very pregnant, me, and Bo-my dog. The first week in the apartment we encountered two major problems. First, we were given an air conditioner that I installed in our living room. It didn't have a front on it because it was purchased at a fire sale and the plastic front had melted. It worked great but looked terrible. The first night I turned it on we were cool as a cucumber until the fan abruptly stopped. We were in bed so I got up to investigate the problem.

I could hear the fan humming as if it wanted to turn but was stuck on something. Because there was no front cover it was easy to reach in to feel what was causing the fan to stick. As soon I reached in I felt some thing against the fan and managed to pull it free. Out came this large BAT that didn't seem happy to have been caught in the fan. The stupid thing dive bombed me as I ran for the bedroom and sure enough he followed me right in. As I dove into the bed, there were Gerry Ellen and Bo already hiding under the blankets. I attempted to push Bo out hoping he would be able to kill that dive-bombing bat. However, he was as scared as us and wouldn't budge an inch.

Here we were Gerry Ellen, Bo, and I all huddled under the blanket as the bat circled the room. Finally I decided that no bat was going to punk me out and waged war. I chased the frantic critter all around the apartment until it finally landed in the corner of the bathroom where I speared it through a wing with our broom handle, impaling it to the wall. The stupid thing squealed a high pitched sound and fluttered its free wing in an attempt to escape and of course Gerry Ellen needed to use the bathroom at that very moment. I had to hold a sheet over her as she used the bathroom just in case the bat got loose. Thankfully the next morning the web-winged intruder was dead.

The second problem came when Bo, who was very jealous of Gerry Ellen, decided to have a showdown with her after I went to work. He chased her on to the kitchen table growling and snapping at her for hours before she was able to get the door open and Bo ran out. As I drove up to our apartment, I thought it was odd that the usual flow of customers weren't coming out of the bank next door or the pizzeria. Suddenly, out of the corner of my eye, there was Bo running up and down the street.

He came running over to lovingly greet me however, I sensed he and I were in deep trouble. When we went up the stairs into the apartment, Bo acted as if he was Gerry Ellen's long lost buddy. Bo's apparent change of heart may have won him an Oscar, but it sure didn't win Gerry Ellen's affections, she gave the ultimatum, it was either Bo or her but one of them was going! I knew I was going to miss my beautiful wife, NOT! JUST KIDDING, JUST KIDDING.

I really missed old Bo, we had been through an awful lot together, and he'd saved my life on numerous occasions.

Living above the Pizzeria also caused a few problems. The local kids gathered there every Saturday night. They would come up the covered stairway which led our apartment to drink beer and smoke Marijuana. That was fine with me however, I informed them that after my wife had our baby they would have to be quiet as they partied outside of the Pizzeria and on our stairway. When Gerry Ellen delivered Robert E. Alexander the II, I told the kids that our baby was home from the hospital and they had to start being quieter.

The first week I warned them three or four times to quiet down or go somewhere else to party. The second weekend my nerves weren't as good and I told them twice to be quiet. The third time, I opened our window which was directly above the Pizzeria door and warned that if they woke my wife and new baby up one more time they would regret it. One of the big shot kids that regularly hung out at the Pizzeria barked, "Shut up and go back to bed you A _ _hole." That was definitely not a wisely chosen remark.

In a flash I jumped into my jeans and bolted down the staircase chasing the kids smoking marijuana and drinking beer all the way to the bottom. As I reached the bottom, three of the teenagers decided that they were going to "Kick my A _ _." That was not a good attitude or the best idea they had ever had either, I dropped the first one who came at me with one punch, grabbed the second one and threw him over the hood of his Volkswagen, then grabbed the third one who by then was trying to escape, and kicked him square in the butt. Then I casually went back up the stairway and crawled into bed again.

Within 20 minutes there was a knock on my door. As I opened it a Deputy Sheriff was standing there. The Deputy asked me what happened because he had been dispatched to a call where a crazy man had attacked the poor innocent local teenagers eating at the Pizzeria. I informed him that I was indeed the man he was looking for, and might be crazy but hadn't attacked any poor innocent teenagers eating anything. I explained that I had warned the kids several times that they were too loud and waking my wife and new born baby. The Deputy told me to come downstairs to talk to the numerous irate parents who wanted me arrested. On the way down the stairs I pointed to half-empty beer bottles and bags of marijuana still on the stairs.

As soon as the parents saw me, they started screaming to have me arrested. A few of the fathers challenged me to a fight which I told them and the Deputy I would be glad to oblige, however, I thought they and the Deputy should at least hear the whole story before I kicked their butts too.

The Deputy interceded and calmed everyone down, convincing the parents to listen to my side of the story before signing a complaint to have me arrested for assault. I told the parents that I had no problem with them having me arrested as long as their kids were tested for alcohol in their blood and also marijuana in their urine. I showed the parents the beer bottles and Marijuana their kids left on my stairwell and told them the entire story. At the end of my story I asked the parents to bring their specific teenager over so I could identify the ones that had been drinking and smoking pot almost every Saturday night for as long as I had lived there.

After the parents questioned their kids and realized that they had indeed been consuming beer along with smoking a little pot, they decided that we were even and didn't want to press charges. I informed them that I would be moving to an apartment in Corfu within a month which was welcomed by all involved.

Shortly after we moved, I was hired as a truck driver by a local concrete company that delivered precast septic tanks and commercial manholes. The salary and medical benefits were very good. Soon, however, Gerry Ellen became pregnant again and realizing that driving a truck was a dead end job, I decided to look for employment with advancement potential.

I saw a notice in the news paper announcing that New York State was offering civil service testing for Correction Officer positions in the prison system. Because I was a Vietnam era veteran and had no criminal record, I was eligible to take the test. I passed receiving a 99.5 out of a 100, and with my veterans credits my score totaled 104.5. I was now rated in the top two percent on the civil service hiring list resulting in my being hired as a New York State Corrections Officer in August, 1973. When my four month training was completed, I was transferred to my permanent position at Attica Correctional Facility. Do you believe it, instead of being incarcerated in Attica; I was going to be a guard there!

CHAPTER 17

THE RAZOR'S EDGE

—⟿—

It was like old home week when I went to work at Attica. I ran into Chuck and James in C Block the second day. Chuck jokingly asked me if I had killed a guard and was trying to escape. The third day I ran into Tommy, who told me he heard I was a Corrections Officer. It was a little awkward at first, however, we all knew the dividing line between COs (Correction Officers) and inmates.

To their credit never once did any of the guys I knew in the streets ever ask for a special favor or for me to break Departmental rules like bringing contraband into the prison. After I was there a few years Chuck and James had their convictions overturned due to legal technicalities and were released. Tommy served over 25 years before being paroled.

I was assigned to be a vacation relief Officer; filling in for COs when they were on vacation. I worked every job on every shift in the prison; oops I can't forget our euphemisms, "Correctional Facility." After the infamous 1971 Attica prison riot the politicians changed the names of prisons and guards to Correctional Facilities and Corrections Officers, however a prison is a prison and a guard is a guard no matter what you try to change the names into. Changing the name of the package doesn't change what is inside!

It didn't take long to realize that even though the salary, health, and retirement benefits were very good, working as a prison guard, while exciting, could also be depressing. You come home from work and your wife asks, "How was your day honey?" You reply, "Well let me see, we had three men raped, four fights, and a small racial confrontation in D Block Recreation Yard. And oh yeah, one inmate sliced his own throat with a tuna can cover, while another hung himself. BUT, no one climbed over the razor wire inner fence and scaled the forty-foot high concrete wall, then slipped past the armed guards and escaped. Boy I had a great day at work!"

It is very safe to say that being employed at a prison offers an extremely unique work environment with each day providing new and challenging situations. Some are brutally gruesome, some perverted, some sad, and some downright hilarious. I will share a few which I believe will take you behind some seriously closed doors, and give you a glimpse of what prison life means.

The prison employed two physicians. Doctor Sternberg, a tall skinny man who looked like Ichabod Crane and spoke with a heavy European accent. He was aggressive and abrupt when examining inmates who signed up to be taken to the prison hospital for sick call each day. One day I was assigned to escort the inmates from A Block to the hospital. When we arrived at the hospital I lined the inmates up single file to be seen by the doctor.

One by one the Doctor Sternberg asked the inmates what was ailing them. As the inmates tried to describe their maladies, he would cut them off and say there was nothing life threatening so they should take an aspirin every four hours and stop wasting his time. The inmates hated Doc Sternberg. As one of the last inmates stepped up to the doctor's table, the Doc in his heavy accent said "Now vhat da H_ _ _ is vrong vith you?" The inmate replied by saying he had a terrible pain in his ear. Doc grabbed the inmates left ear yanking his head side ways as he told the inmate that he didn't see anything wrong.

The inmate told him that it was the other ear that had the pain. Doc instantly grabbed the inmate's left ear again yanking his head around glancing at the ear. Within a second of glancing into the left ear Doc again said that he didn't see anything wrong "vwat-so-ever." The inmate indigently complained that the pain was first, very deep, and second, in the other ear! Doc grabbed the right ear this time, and as he pulled the inmate halfway over the table exclaimed that he could see right through to the other side and nothing was wrong. The inmate again insisted that there was a terrible pain deep in his right ear.

At that point Doc, his eyes bulging in disdain yelled at the inmate "Who da H_ _ _ do you think is the doctor here, me or you?" Immediately the inmate curtly replied, "As good as you are, I might as well be the doctor!" Doc went nuts cursing and yelling for me to get the G_ _ D_ _ _ blankety, blank inmate out of his hospital and to lock this Son of a B_ _ _ _ up! To lock up an inmate meant to lock him in his cell until he was interviewed by the disciplinary adjustment committee because of an incident. The disciplinary adjustment committee would punish the inmate with more time locked in his cell usually up to two weeks. Actually, I thought that inmate made an astute observation of the doctor's ability and shouldn't be locked up at all.

The other prison doctor, Doc Williams was fairly reasonable with the inmates and great to the guards. When we would come into work with hangovers he would brew up a little potion of Belladonna, Kaopectate, and a few other drugs which he told us to slowly sip. It worked wonders within two hours we felt like a million bucks ready to finish out the day and start drinking all over again.

I will share another funny incident. I was in charge of the "Coal Gang," which consisted of 20 inmates who were assigned to shovel coal out of railroad cars brought in to the prison to supply the coal for the power house. The power house provided heat and hot water for the prison. In the summertime I assigned the inmates to mow the grass on the side of the hill that the railroad tracks were on. I always demanded that inmates wear steel covers over their shoes when cutting the grass to protect their feet from the blades of the lawnmower.

One morning as two inmates were mowing the grass on the side of the hill I heard a blood curtailing scream from their vicinity. Sure enough, one of the inmates, who was not wearing foot protectors had just slipped and pulled the mower on top of his left foot. After grabbing a towel from my office I ran to the inmate who was tightly grasping his foot. I told him to let go of his foot so I could wrap it in the towel. However, he refused to release his death grip and kept screaming that all of his toes had been cut off. I called the hospital asking for a nurse to come to the coal yard as soon as possible to treat and transport an inmate who had possibly cut the toes off of his left foot.

While we were waiting for the medical staff to arrive I tried to calm the frantic inmate down fearing he may go into shock. I couldn't see if he had indeed cut his toes off or not so I tried to get a look at his foot and wrap it with a towel. I finally got him to calm down by telling him that I could see toes and that he probably only lacerated them. The ruse didn't work, he still wouldn't let go of his foot so I could see the actual damage. He kept apologizing to me for taking the foot protectors off and begging me not to remove him from the coal gang.

Finally the nurse showed up with a gurney to take him to the hospital. After we placed the inmate on the gurney the nurse told the inmate to loosen his hands so he could administer first aid to his foot. At first the inmate refused saying that he couldn't feel any toes and that they were probably all gone, however, with the nurse and me coaxing him, he finally loosened his grip. I blocked his view as the nurse carefully removed his hand from around the foot. At that instant one of the other coal gang inmates named Manny leaned over the gurney and announced, "Oh my God they're all gone." The inmate freaked out screaming and yelling as he was rushed to the hospital.

I told the other coal gang inmates to hurry to the site of the accident to see if they could find any toes, hoping if any were found they might be reattached. The search came up empty and by then it was time for me to escort them to their cells in B Block to prepare for the noon meal. I then went to C Block to wait for the tear gas to be brought to the observation areas over looking the mess halls. I manned the tear gas booth in A Mess Hall during both the morning and noon meals.

As I sat in the gas booth I received a telephone call from the guard in wall tower # 7 explaining that he had good and bad news. The good news was that he could see the toes, the bad news was that the many cats that inhabit the prison grounds were eating them. After escorting the inmates back to the coal yard after lunch, we immediately ran to the spot where the guard saw the cats having their noon meal on the toes.

After an intense search all that was found was the half eaten big toe. I told the inmates to dispose of the toe by putting it in a bag and burning it in the incinerator. However, one of the Native American inmates took the toe to his cell and that night made a beaded necklace with the big-toe bone on it. The next morning he gave me the necklace which I decided might lift up the spirits of the injured inmate who was now in the prison ward at Erie County Medical Center in Buffalo. I talked one of the transport Officers in to taking the necklace to the inmate when he made the daily trip to transport inmates to and from the hospital.

The injured inmate recovered and was discharged form the Erie County Medical Center, returning to the prison within a week. The morning after the he was returned to Attica, I was stopped at the front gate of the prison and ordered to immediately report to the Deputy Superintendent of Security's office. When I entered his office, Deputy Superintendent Curtis asked me if I knew anything about a necklace containing the big-toe bone of my injured coal gang inmate. It seams that the inmate refused to give up the necklace when he reentered the prison and caused a major scene as the guards tried to take it from him.

Of course I denied any knowledge of such a necklace or how it would have been delivered to the inmate at Erie County Medical Center. Deputy Superintendent Curtis with his raspy voice ordered me to deposit the toe necklace in the inmate's personal property only to be given to him if and when he was paroled. He then sternly ordered me out of his office. As I headed toward the door Curtis, with a chuckle declared, "Alexander that it was the d_ _ _dest thing I've ever seen in my 30 years working in prisons."

We filled the injured man's position on the coal gang with another inmate who immediately caught my attention. He had an Animal Motorcycle Gang tattoo on his extremely scarred arm. The Animals Motor Cycle gang was located in Niagara Falls and was rivals of the KingsMen. When I asked him how he received all the scars on his arms, neck and face, he shared a story about being jumped by large group of blankety, blank, blank KingsMen. He also opened his shirt to show many scars from being cut and stabbed in the chest during the vicious attack which almost took his life.

When he finished his story I said that it wasn't true. He boldly challenged me as to how I would know anything about the matter. I then told him exactly what happened. He had stabbed a KingsMen in the Hell's Angels Club house in Buffalo. In retaliation a group of KingsMen rolled on up to Niagara Falls finding him and other members of the Animals in a bar in the marketplace alley.

The KingsMen *did* storm the place brandishing shot-guns, however, a *group* of KingsMen *did not* attack him. The way it played out was that I held him down while two other KingsMen, Tommy and Little Joe, stabbed and cut him. His eyes were wide open in shock as I asked him if he wanted to be taken off the coal gang. He said he could handle it shook my hand and said let bygones be bygones. He also knew that I could inform the other inmates that he was incarcerated for raping his young stepdaughters, a crime that would bring the wrath of other inmates upon him. There was nothing worse than child abusers which other inmates disdainfully referred to as "baby-bangers." It may be hard to understand, but child abusers were viewed as giving inmates in general a "bad name." Those inmates who were convicted of raping children were castigated and even targeted for rape themselves.

There was an inmate Mike Casella who worked on the coal gang. He was a short stocky guy who always had a funny comment or two. He was pick axing coal from with in the frozen Rail road cars on a frigid January day, when the coal broke loose crashing down and out of the bottom of the coal car and on to a conveyor belt that went into the prison Power House. Unfortunately Mike slipped and went down the coal shute with the coal. I was sure he would be ground to pieces as I ran to the door of the Power House anticipated a gory scene. I repeatedly rang the doorbell as I waited for what seemed like an eternity for the civilian in charge to open the door. I exhorted him to hurry because inmate Casella had gone down the coal shute and on the conveyor belt. As he opened the door he asked why I was in such a hurry when Casella would surely be dead, "Probably chewed to bits."

As I ran toward the stairway which led to the basement of the Power House I couldn't believe my eyes, there came Casella with his shirt and pants torn and tattered and his body completely covered in thick black coal dust from head to toe. When I got with in ten feet of him I could see small lines of blood all over his body that were oozing through the coal dust. Stunned, I exclaimed "Mike your alive!" His reply, "What a rush boss, what a rush!" Except for the fifty or so small cuts caused by the sharp corners of the coal as he tumbled along the conveyor belt he was in good condition.

The last incident I will share is indelibly etched on my mind. One day I was asked to work a double shift so I headed over to C Block where I would work the second eight hours. When I entered the third floor control room the inmates were coming in from the recreation yard. I opened the cells as the inmates called out their cell numbers. In C Block there were 42 cells facing each other on the galleries, meaning that there were up to 84 inmates out of their cells at any one time. On this afternoon there were approximately 60 inmates returning from the yard.

As I was opening the cells I noticed a commotion at the far end of the gallery. Inmates started yelling "Fight!" causing many to rush toward the end of the gallery to see what was going on. Many times small fights escalate into major disturbances especially if two racial groups are engaged in an altercation. I turned to John who was the other officer assigned to the control cage alerting him that I had a fight at the end of my gallery. As I left the safety of the control cage and headed down the gallery toward the fight, I assumed that John would immediately declare an emergency and call for back-up.

I ordered the inmates into their cells, however, many were reluctant to go in so I pushed them slamming their cell doors, attempting to prevent a more serious emergency from developing. At one point as I was approximately halfway down the gallery an inmate drop kicked me in the back knocking me into an open cell.

For a fleeting moment I considered closing the cell door and staying there until the back up officers arrived. I remember thinking, "Bob, God hates a coward, and *this* is what they pay me for," as I jumped up and charged out of the cell. Briefly turning back toward the control cage, I yelled "John, John, where is the back up?" then continued to force inmates into cells. As I approached the combatants at the end of the gallery where the fight was raging, I realized it was between a Hispanic and a white inmate, whose back was toward me. A small group of white and Hispanic inmates had gathered around the brawl.

Just as I was about to grab the white inmate from behind I saw him raise a weapon made out of razor blades melted into a tooth brush handle and thrust it down the forehead and nose of the Hispanic inmate. At that very instant the point of a home made dagger came through the back of the white inmate's neck, almost penetrating my nose. As I spun him around, blood from a severed artery in his neck squirted directly into my eyes.

I slipped on the blood falling to the floor, and in all the commotion felt the inmate being pulled away from me. I tried desperately to wipe my eyes so I could see, expecting to be stabbed at any moment. When I finally was able to see again there were only four or five Hispanic inmates on the gallery one bleeding profusely, still holding the dagger in his hand. All the white inmates, including the one stabbed through the neck, were gone.

I ordered the Hispanic inmates to get a towel from a cell so I could put it on the wounds of the injured inmate. At that moment he tossed the dagger into an open cell where another inmate threw it out the window. The fact that the dagger was now out of the scene convinced me that I would probably come out of this situation alive. I couldn't believe that back-up officers hadn't responded to the emergency. I was given a towel which I put against the inmate's face and I, along with two other inmates, hurriedly brought him back up the gallery. As we approached the staircase I could hear guards come running up the stairs. When they saw the amount of blood on me they thought I had been stabbed.

I assured them I was okay as they helped me take the injured inmate to the hospital. I was told that John had not reported the fight over the intercom and that they didn't realize anything was happening on the third floor until five inmates came down the stairs carrying a severely wounded man with blood squirting from his neck. When I came back to C block from the hospital and confronted John as to why he hadn't declared the fight or the emergency, he responded by saying that it seemed that I had things under control. Wouldn't you know, a week later he was promoted to Sergeant!

I inquired as to the fate of the inmate with the neck wound and was told that he had been transported to a Batavia hospital for emergency treatment and then taken to Erie County Medical Center. Amazingly both inmates survived. The white inmate sued the Department of Corrections and me personally for $2 million claiming that I was hesitant and didn't respond to the fight fast enough. Oh by the way, the fight was over the Hispanic inmate not paying for a quart of home made potato wine. After three years the suit was dismissed.

Many prison guards were or became alcoholics. I decided that I needed to develop options other than being a Hack, (the term inmates referred to guards as) if I was going to work in the system for an entire twenty-five or thirty year career. Because I had served four years in the Air Force I was entitled to Veterans benefits to attend college. For the next nine years I worked full time at Attica Prison while attending college full time at night. I enrolled in Genesee Community College studying Criminal Justice receiving an Associates Degree in

Correctional Administration. I then transferred to the prestigious Rochester Institute of Technology (RIT) where I graduated with honors, receiving my Bachelors Degree in Criminal Justice. That was followed by a Masters Degree in Counseling from Canisius College in Buffalo, another highly acclaimed academic institution. I also completed two years of Graduate study in Governmental Administration at the State University of New York at Brockport.

When I received my Bachelors Degree from RIT it was a special and emotional day for me. I was the first Alexander to not only graduate from high school but also from college. It was the first time any member of my family had attended one of my graduation ceremonies, even Mom, Dad, and Ed were in attendance, though Mom did sit far away from Dad.

As I was handed my diploma, I couldn't help but feel I owed part of my degree to the inmates I used as laboratory specimens to test the psychological and sociological theories I learned in college. Among my specimens was David Berkowitz, the notorious "Son of Sam" murderer from New York City.

During the time I worked and attended college, Gerry Ellen and I had four more children, Jennifer, nicknamed Jenny, (who I named after my favorite beer, Genesee Beer), Twin boys, Brian and Brandon, and another girl, Brandi, (who I named after my favorite mixed drink, a Brandy Alexander).

What was amazing was that I was able to keep my alcoholism as the center of my life while working full time, attending college for nine years, and becoming involved with civic and other organizations. I became a Cub Scout Master, worked with the Boy Scouts, ran for and was elected to the Pembroke High School Board of Education. Within two years I became the Vice President of the board and was its President for six years.

The troubled kid who was tagged a looser and incorrigible, the one who was expelled for switching papers to expose the hypocrisy of the cast system, the rebel who signed those immortal words "Kiss my A_ _, I do so declare," on the New York Regents Examinations in 1963, was now the President of the Board of Education. I ran for the Board of Education with a vendetta to fire that albatross of a counselor that told Charlie and me that we were too stupid to go to college.

Well not really, however, I did have an ulterior motive, to work to develop systems in the public schools that understood the Bobby Alexander's of the world. I hoped to develop model programs for schools to identify and address the needs of kids who, like me, had no family support system. I also knew that by being on the board my children were going to receive what I didn't, a legitimate opportunity to excel.

At the Prison I was promoted to Correction Counselor. I was elected Union President of our Attica Prison Professionals Union, the Public Employees Federation. I was also elected to the State Wide Labor Management Committee which represented all the professional employees working in the entire New York State Prison system. I ended up being the Chairman of that Committee for four years. Additionally, I was trained to be on the Hostage Negotiation Crisis Intervention Team, the first responders and negotiators in prison emergencies.

Many members of the local community were very impressed by my resume which included being on the Board of Education, a Cub Scout Leader, Baseball Coach in the Pembroke Youth Athletic Association, Union President, State Wide Labor Management Chair, and Crisis Intervention Team Leader. I also was hired as an Adjunct Faculty member for Genesee Community College and my alma mater, Rochester Institute of Technology (RIT), teaching Criminal Justice, Psychology, and Sociology courses.

My life was like a circus; I worked from 8 to 4 at the Prison, and then on the way home hurriedly stopped at Jimmy K's bar or the Val Hal La for three or four quick drinks. I usually drank brandy and milk because my stomach was in poor shape from twenty-five years of alcohol abuse. After a couple draft beer chasers I would zoom home to grab a bite of dinner before heading off for the night's events.

Gerry Ellen was my life saver, always having dinner waiting as well as keeping track of what meeting I was scheduled for or what college and course I was teaching on any given night. Because I was the State Wide labor Management Committee Chairman I only worked three days a week and had two days for union business. During each year I traveled across New York State visiting most of the over fifty Correctional facilities. I also met with the Commissioner of Correctional Services, Thomas Coughlin III and/or his staff in Albany New York every few weeks.

An example of a typical few days for me might give you a glimpse of how hectic it was. I might work at my job at Attica on Monday, from 8 to 4, stopping for a few quick drinks on my way home; eat dinner, then drive the hour it took to get to RIT where I taught from 6 to 9:30p.m. After teaching I'd down a few drinks with my colleagues as we solved the world's problems, drive the hour it took to get home, sleep a few hours, and catch a plane at 7 a.m. to fly to Albany. I would then meet with Commissioner Coughlin at 9:30 a.m., followed by a meeting with his staff for another hour, contact union leaders at numerous facilities, and fly back to Buffalo. I would rush home, eat dinner, and then hurry out the door to attend a school board meeting. After the meeting and a few drinks with the Superintendent, I would return home for a few hours sleep, get up, and start all over again.

To add to the equation, almost every Saturday I played softball, drank, and fought at the Val Hal La just to keep in shape.

Chapter 18

After all these years

—〰—

To describe Gerry Ellen and pay adequate tribute to how she survived is almost impossible. However, I will explain what she experienced, conquered, and still overcomes today. Are there issues and scars she still struggles with, certainly, however, her faith in Christ Jesus and His unconditional love gives her the ability to press on.

Gerry Ellen's father was an alcoholic whose entire life revolved around frequenting local watering holes. Psychologically abused by her mother, she was forced to excel at everything she did, yet never received positive reinforcement. In fact, if she completed tasks perfectly she was told she had to do better. Can you imagine getting a perfect 100 percent on a school test then be told it wasn't good enough.

Her spirit was mercilessly attacked and she was kept from showing emotions, especially when it came to giving or receiving all-embracing love. She certainly never experienced unconditional love, and in fact those two words weren't even in her vocabulary. Being held to standards no one could attain was bad enough, but Gerry Ellen was further crushed when she was viciously attacked those few times she was allowed to open up emotionally.

The lesson, in no uncertain terms, was that she could never allow herself to become vulnerable and, if she did, horrible repercussions were sure to follow. What was so terribly sad was that her mother believed that the brutal attacks were actually nurturing and protecting Gerry Ellen by programming her to succeed and survive in a "harsh and cruel world." It was like she was being served a bitter dinner with arsenic for dessert.

At 15, she was ripped from the only partially stable environment she knew when her parents sold their home in Buffalo and bought a bar in rural Indian Falls, New York. The move created a serious problem, because her parents were planning to live in the bar until they generated enough profit to buy or build a home, there was no room for Gerry Ellen. She was shipped off to live with her sister Kathy. And just when she had adjusted to her new life, Kathy's daughter was diagnosed with Cystic Fibrosis and she was again rejected and sent to live with her other sister Sandy. Ironically, within a few months, however, she was sent back to live with Kathy again.

She had four children including a set of twin boys before she was 20 years old, raising them while I worked and attended college for nine years. She also was burdened with caring for and refereeing the war between her mother and my mother, both of whom lived with us for over 20 years.

I must explain how her mother ended up living with us. After Eddie wrecked the bar and left Ma holding the bag, she sold the place and bought a horse farm with her sister and brother-in-law. Ma covered the down payment to buy the farm and her sister was to pay the remaining mortgage. They would share the house until an apartment would be built for Ma.

Within two years her sister gave Ma $6,000 and threw her off the farm. The deed had been drafted in her sister's name because Ma had trusted her, thus she had no recourse and was essentially homeless. Her children, Sandy, Kathy, and Eddie Jr. all refused to take her in. No one would want to live with Ma. No one that is except Gerry Ellen whose tender heart led her to ask me if Ma could live with us.

Her sisters implored us not to take her in, saying she would wreck our marriage and continue to abuse Gerry Ellen. They were flabbergasted that she would even consider allowing Ma to live with her. They had witnessed the terrible abuse heaped on Gerry Ellen, an abuse even more severe than they had experienced. However, Gerry Ellen and I agreed that we couldn't just throw her away and abandon her, even if she deserved it. Someone had to show her mercy despite the fact that she had never shown it to anyone else.

Ma lived with us for a year while I built her an apartment attached to our house. It wasn't easy having Ma with us, she browbeat and played every head game possible in an attempt to control Gerry Ellen. After she was in her own domain behind our house, conditions improved a little and at least we could escape from her by locking our door when she was at her worst.

Another phenomenon developed while Ma lived with us; transference. Ma transferred the disdain and belittlement she had at one time viciously attacked Ed senior with, onto me. There wasn't anything I did that was right or good. She attacked me every time she had an opportunity, especially to my children.

When my mother moved into the apartment it was like a war every day between them. Grandma Gert was loving, kind, and a playmate to our children, and they adored her for it. Ma was always furious at the children when they would go back to the apartment to see Grandma Gert. She was consumed with a jealously firing a continuous barrage of verbal assaults against Grandma Gert and the kids.

During the best of times it was only a little less than a cold war atmosphere. What was interesting was that the kids loved both Ma and Grandma Gert, sorting out the situation and dealing with each Grandmother separately in an understanding way. While doing their best to ignore their Grandmothers' raging war, they enjoyed each separately learning how to cook, sew, and make crafts with Grandma DuPont, while playing with Grandma Gert as if she was their peer.

How Gerry Ellen survived taking care of six children, a high-functioning alcoholic husband, while refereeing the deep conflict between her Mother and Mother-in-law is a testimony to her inner strength and perseverance. I know of no other person who could survive such a hostile and depressing environment. Do you believe in miracles? Do you believe that God ordains events in our lives?

Eddie got saved and began witnessing to the entire family and I mean the entire family. When he approached me, one of the first things he shared was that when I witnessed to him those many years before as we sat on the rocks watching the sun come up, God planted a seed that later was watered by his wife and her brother, then God reaped the harvest. He hugged and thanked me for being so bold as to share Jesus with him and then begged me to come back to Jesus myself. Every one in the family rejected the message of the cross, even me who had shared it with him years before. I didn't think God could or would forgive me for all the terrible things I had done. I loved alcohol more than anything else- it was my god because it numbed my soul as I wallowed in pain, rage, and guilt.

About this time an event occurred that I wasn't sure ever would. I knew my maternal Mother's name was Margaret Ingersoll because Aunt Adeline had told me when I left for the Vietnam War. One day I was asked to work overtime at the prison. I decided to mosey down to the 3 to 11 shift roll call even though I knew I was going to work at "Time Square" in the center of the prison. Normally when you are working over time you just reported to the assigned area at 3 o'clock.

At the roll call, I was shocked to hear the name Ingersoll when the sergeant called out the names of the guards. Niles Ingersoll worked in 8-Post on the wall surrounding the prison. My heart pounded as I contemplated the possibility that Niles Ingersol could be my Mother's husband. And if he was, I couldn't help but wonder if he knew I existed, and how would he react if I contacted her.

I asked the other guard assigned to Times Square if he knew Niles Ingersoll's wife's name. He didn't know her name but did tell me that she and Niles sold real estate. As thoughts and emotions raced through my mind I summoned up the courage to call 8-Post and asked Niles what his wife's first name was and he replied Marge. Instantly my emotions deflated thinking, false alarm, then Niles corrected himself and said, "Her real name is Margaret, but we just call her Marge."

He then asked if I was interested in real estate to which I replied, "Yes." Questions and fear again raced through my mind, "Should I even try to meet her to see if she was my Mother? What if she wasn't my mother? If she was my Mother would she want to see me? What if she rejected me? Would I cause her and or any of her family pain?" After the mind boggling fretting and anguish over the possible outcomes I came to the decision that I had to know no matter what the consequences. I had the perfect venue to check her out without her knowing who I was; I was just interested in real estate.

There were a few clues I could interject into a conversation to help me discern if I had found my Mother. It had been 30 years since she adopted me out so she would be 45 years old. She had grown up in Sheldon, New York as a young girl, and lived with my Aunt Adeline and Uncle Ed while she was pregnant with me. I anxiously anticipated the moment that I would know if this Margaret Ingersoll was indeed my Mother, and if so, how I would tell her who I was.

I called the Sergeant in charge of the 3 to 11 shift telling him I had become ill and needed to go home. I also called Niles asking him where he lived and if his wife might be home. He gave me the address and directions and said she indeed would be home.

After what seemed like an eternity a guard finally arrived to relieve me and away I went to the Ingersoll home which was just around the corner from the prison. My heart was in my throat as I rang the doorbell. When the door opened, I was greeted by a young man who identified himself as Mark. He immediately asked if I was there to talk to his Mother about real estate and I replied, "I certainly am." He invited me in as he told me his Mother would be right back from the store. As we sat in the living room I wondered if this teenage boy was my brother. With in a few minutes Marge returned and Mark introduced me as Mr. Alexander who was looking for real estate, then left the room.

Here I was sitting across from the woman who could be my Mother. I struggled to suppress the fear of possible rejection, and the crushing weight of anticipating this moment for so many years. I gained control of my emotions and focused on the deception of searching for real estate while discreetly asking questions that would give me a clue as to whether this woman was indeed my Mother.

As we looked at photographs of homes I asked if the pictures on her piano and walls were of her family and thankfully she fell for the trap pointing out who each of her five children were and gave me a synopsis of their lives. I asked if she had lived in Attica all her life and felt shivers up and down my spine when she replied that she was raised in the Sheldon, New York area, right where Aunt Adeline had told me she was had lived.

With in 20 minutes I was positive I was talking to my Mother. As I was about to tell her that she was talking to the child she had given away all those years ago, fear flooded my heart. What if she rejected me and ordered me out of her house declaring that she never wanted to see me now or ever again? I wasn't sure if I could handle another rejection, especially from my real Mother.

I almost chickened out and got up to leave. However, as she closed her real estate book, I told her that I thought she knew someone I knew to which she replied, "Who?" When I said, "Ed and Adeline Theon," she stared at me stunned for a moment and with tears welling up in her eyes asked, "Are you Bobby?" I softly answered, "Yes I am." Trying to be gracious, I told her that if she didn't want me to bother her, I would leave immediately and never contact her again.

Marge was visibly shaken but told me that she didn't want me to leave. She explained that except for her Mother, no one in her family knew I existed, including her five children. Again I reassured her that I didn't want to cause her any pain or trouble, and so I would leave and let her think it over before deciding what she wanted to do. She started to tell me why she had to give me up and how she agonized when she read the notice of John and Gertrude Faulring's divorce in the newspaper. Tears streamed down her face as she explained how she was devastated by their divorce and wanted to find and bring me home to live with her.

It was obvious she felt extremely guilty for giving me up and painfully asked if I hated her for giving me away. I softly answered, "I don't hate you at all; you gave me life." I gave her my address and telephone number telling her I wouldn't contact her again and that any interaction would be on her terms, if at all.

The next day when I came home from work she called, still shaken and with her voice trembling asked, "Can I come over and meet your wife and children." I told her to come right over. After a tearful introduction to Gerry Ellen and the kids we sat and talked for hours. She shared that she had made a vow to see me before she died and wondered if she was about to die. I didn't know if she was about to die but I could feel the deep seated pain and guilt haunting her.

She then asked me if I would allow her to introduce me to her family at a party she would like to have at her home. Marge had talked to her family telling them about me and they were all anxious to meet me and my family. We had the welcoming and introduction party a few weeks later. It was a very emotional day as I was officially introduced to my half-brothers, Niles Junior, who everyone called Skip, Mark, and Scott, along with my half-sisters, Patty and Jo Ann, along with a host of new aunts, uncles, and cousins.

It seemed strange and a little uncomfortable meeting my Grandmother and her husband Fritz, who was still a vile alcoholic. She had kept the secret of my birth and didn't want anyone to know I existed, so I couldn't help but wonder how she felt about me contacting my mother. I also wondered what Niles felt like down deep inside. The whole introduction process was a little overwhelming for everyone; however, it was a good beginning.

CHAPTER 19

THE GATES OF HELL SHALL
NOT PREVAIL

—ⴣⴣⴣ—

In 1980 I became a counselor at the prison. Of the 12 counselors in the counseling unit, I was the only one with a
Master's Degree in counseling; in fact I was the only one
with any degree in counseling at all. The other counselors
had an assortment of degrees including: computers, business, and model making. But my supervisor topped them all;
he had a bachelor's degree in animal husbandry! Think what
you want, but I wouldn't take my cow to a counselor or an
inmate to a veterinarian, even if some people suggest that
veterinarians are appropriate for convicted felons.

I was assigned to a caseload of over 125 inmates whose
inmate number ended in eight. Inmates are assigned to
counselors by the last digit in their New York State Prison
identification number. Consider David Berkowitz's inmate
number, 78-A-1976. The 78 stands for the year he came into
the prison system, while the A designates the Downstate
Reception and Classification Center where he was processed.
In 1978 David was the 1,976[th] inmate processed that year.

There was a counselor assigned to handle inmates incarcerated in what is called *Segregation*, also referred to as the

Special Housing Unit (SHU). At Attica, SHU was located in the Reception Building far removed from the general population. It housed two kinds of inmates: disciplinary problems and offenders like David Berkowitz and Mark David Chapman who were designated as Administrative Protective Custody Inmates. They were placed there because the Administration felt they were in danger of being assaulted or killed due to the notoriety of their crimes.

In David's case even being in SHU didn't stop him from being attacked. His throat was sliced while he worked in the Special Housing Unit as a porter cleaning the gallery in front of the disciplinary cells. David never said who attacked him, however, I knew exactly who it was. The attacker was an inmate who once worked on my Coal Gang and vowed to kill David Berkowitz if he ever had the chance. Sure enough, his cell in disciplinary segregation was right where David was attacked.

I wound up working SHU because the counselor who was assigned to the segregation units experienced a little problem; an inmate housed in a disciplinary cell threw a bucket of urine and fecal matter in his face. He was reassigned back to the general counseling unit and I was asked to cover segregation until a permanent counselor was assigned. I was condescendingly told that I could use my master's degree in counseling on the disciplinary inmates. My supervisor laughingly bellowed "Maybe your degree will prevent you from being dowsed with urine and fecal matter." He was right! I utilized many of the skills learned while gaining my master's degree in counseling to defuse countless situations that could have easily escalated into violent confrontations or urine and fecal showers.

As I began to counsel Mark David Chapman, the man who shot John Lennon, I never would have dreamed how God would use him to bring my wife to salvation.

During the first counseling session with Mark, he told me he was a Christian. I immediately thought, "Yeah, right, my Grandmother was a Christian." My guess was that Mark had become what we described as a "Jail House Conversion". That's when a convicted criminal gets religion hoping God will intercede, protect, and ultimately help him look good to the Parole Board. I laughed to myself thinking that Mark had 20 years before he even saw the Parole Board.

I had experienced hundreds of jail house conversions where inmates attend church services regularly, joined Bible studies run by the prison chaplain or by outside Christian groups. These inmates run all over the prison praising God claiming they "talk the talk," and are "walking the walk," in other words talking Jesus talk and walking the Christian walk. However, as soon as they walked out the front gate after making parole, they threw their Bible up in the air and headed back to their life of sin and crime as fast as they could.

I will share one horrific story of one such inmate and the disaster he caused. The inmate attended every church service and every Bible study, and even had Jesus posters in his cell. He continually told the guards that he was praying for them. He also joined a Bible study held by a local church group twice a month.

Unfortunately this inmate was able to con the wife of a member of the church Bible group into thinking she was most wonderful person he had ever met. He also said that he couldn't help it but he knew God had brought them together for a purpose and that he had fallen in love with her. In reality, he saw a sucker whose low self-esteem made her an easy prey for his manipulations.

By the time the Bible study husband realized there was something going on between his wife and the inmate it was too late; she was hooked. She left her husband and filed for divorce. After her divorce she came to the prison daily to visit the "soul mate" God had brought her way. Because any inmate requesting to be married has to meet with his counselor and bride-to-be, I met with them. The reason for the mandatory meeting was to explain exactly what the inmate was convicted of and how long he would be incarcerated. This was mandatory because many prisoners were less than truthful about their crimes and possible release date.

Of course before I could begin to explain this inmate's crimes and parole hearing date she informed me that he had explained everything including his innocence and being framed for the crime he was convicted of. I knew it was a futile to try to convince her that it would be better to wait until the inmate was released from prison, established a residency, and procured employment before they were married. She became a little indignant and retorted that God had brought them together and they were going to serve him for the remaining time he was in prison and establish a Christian outreach for paroled inmates after he was released.

The lady called me at least three times a week trying to hurry the process for their marriage made in prison, oops, Heaven. I tried my absolute best to convince her to wait to marry him and explained that she may find a different reality after he was paroled, one she may not have expected. The inmate threatened to file a grievance against me for holding up the process for their marriage. He was right; I was guilty of holding up the process for as long as I could.

After the loving couple was married I often saw them in the visiting room holding hands and planning their post-parole ministry. Within six months he was paroled. I wish I could report that they are still ministering to parolees; however, the tragic truth is sickening. I received a call from the lady who with a drug-slurred voice and sobbing told me I was right and that she should have listened to me. She begged me to continue trying to convince other women who want to marry their "prison soul mate," to wait and time-test them as I had begged her to do.

As she wept she shared that the Christian outreach to parolees was actually an invitation to have sex with her. Upon release he had continually beaten her and his friends repeatedly raped and sodomized her. He also forced her into becoming a prostitute and a heroin addict to seal her fate and prevent her from trying to escape. She was calling to also tell me to never let Christian women participate in men's prison Bible studies. When she finished she told me she was about to commit suicide. Before I could say a word the line went dead.

There were inmates that married their pen pals who usually were psychologically co-dependant women looking to be rescued by rescuing those in desperate need. Of course many ended up being abused and locked into a relationship far more disastrous than they had originally endured. Some of them were even murdered. I remember one inmate who called from the Protestant Chaplin's office to have his prison bride murdered for the life insurance money. He convinced her that they needed the security of a large life insurance policy so that if either one of them happened to die, the other would be taken care of. He sure took care of her.

So you can understand why, when Mark David Chapman claimed he was a Christian, I wasn't especially impressed. However, I did enjoy counseling him and also meeting his wife Gloria who moved to the local area to be near him. Mark had an affable way about himself, and anyone getting to know him couldn't help but like him. He was diligent at performing his porter duties and soon was picked to assist the guards serving food to the inmates in disciplinary segregation.

If there was one trait everyone immediately recognized Mark for, it was perfection. Mark strived for perfection at everything he did. I won't share any specifics about the issues Mark and I discussed and worked on, because even though many of them are public knowledge, I would never risk breaking the professional counselor/client relationship. I will only say that we developed a strong bond and were confronting some of his major personal issues.

When a new counselor was assigned to replace me as counselor of the Special Housing Unit, Mark requested that I remain his individual counselor which my supervisor approved. I was assigned a new caseload of inmates including Mark. As we progressed in our interaction I realized that Mark was an extremely complex person and that I would be challenged to utilize every bit of skill I possessed to work with him.

One afternoon after work I stopped at Jimmy K's bar for a few drinks and a game of euchre. This was one of the few times I actually had nothing to do at night. I stayed at the bar until about 7:30 p.m. and then went home. I entered the house to find Gerry Ellen washing the dinner dishes and keeping my meal warm on the stove. As I went in to change my clothes, she asked me if I would turn off the television, which the kids had left on when they headed out side to terrorize the neighborhood.

She commented that she could hear the Billy Graham crusade being televised and that she couldn't stand that crazy, screaming Protestant minister. As I went to the living room to shut the TV off, I remembered how much Gram and Mom loved Billy Graham, and George Beverly Shay's beautiful deep voice singing "His eye is on the sparrow, and I know he watches me."

Just as I reached down to turn it off a message appeared on the screen, "For Prayer, Call This Number." I ran into the kitchen grabbed a piece of paper and pen and ran back to the television to write the prayer number down. As I hurriedly returned to the kitchen and picked up the phone to dial the number, Gerry Ellen sarcastically asked "What are you doing?" I told her Mark claimed to be a Christian and I was an eclectic counselor so I thought maybe the Billy Graham folks would have some materials I could use when counseling him. Gerry Ellen asked if I had flipped my lid, and if I was crazy. Maybe I was crazy, but I knew I just had to call that number. What I didn't know was that the call I was about to make was orchestrated by God, not for Mark David Chapman but for Gerry Ellen Alexander.

When the lady answered the phone and asked what my prayed request was, I informed her that I was counselor at Attica prison and working with a world famous murderer who claimed to be a Christian. I asked if they had some Christian materials that might help me. I think the poor lady prayed for herself first, then for me, and the inmate. She asked for my address and thanked me for calling.

As I said before, God works in strange and mighty ways His wonders to perform. I went back to work the next day only to have Mark tell me he didn't want me for a counselor any more. He claimed I had shared information about him and his wife, Gloria, with a magazine and had put her life in jeopardy. I told him I would never do such a terrible thing. Mark challenged me to prove it, to which I responded that on my word as a professional counselor, I did not contact any magazine. He then replied that my word wasn't enough and he wanted a new counselor, which my supervisor granted.

An amazing sequence of events that would change our lives forever was about to take place. When I came home I told Gerry Ellen that I wasn't counseling Mark anymore yet two days later an envelope arrived from The Billy Graham Evangelical Association. Gerry Ellen knew I wouldn't need the material because Mark had another counselor. She sure wouldn't need it and certainly didn't want any of that Protestant propaganda from crazy Billy Graham lying around the house, so she promptly tossed it into the garbage can. She may have thought she was rid of Billy Graham, but God had other plans. Every time she walked past the garbage can she was drawn to retrieve the now soiled envelope. Finally, she gave in.

As she opened the envelope and pulled out an enclosed booklet, she asked herself, "What in the world am I doing?" At that moment she was holding the Gospel of John. She didn't realize it, but God was about to change her life. My little wife sat down and read John 1:1, "In the beginning was the Word and the Word was with God and the Word was God." Then in verse 14, "The Word became flesh and dwelt among us." She read John 3:3 declaring that she needed to be born again. As she pondered what "being born again might mean," she was drawn and read the entire Gospel of John. For the first time she realized that Jesus Christ came from Heaven to earth to shed His blood for her sin once and for all. Gerry Ellen was amazed to discover that she couldn't work her way to Heaven hoping she had been good enough to get in; salvation was free, a gift paid for by the precious blood of Jesus Christ on Calvary's cross. Falling to her knees, she repented and asked Jesus to forgive her of her sin and to please come into her heart.

I have traveled the United States and Canada sharing my testimony. Every time I speak, I warn men that if their wives who have a religion get saved, beginning a personal relationship with the King of Kings and Lord of Lords, give up because they don't shut up! They just keep praying for you. My wife began to pray for me that day and continued without ceasing for over three years. The woman who had been at my side in bars for 14 years through brawls, shootings, and tirades now refused to set foot in one.

She also started two practices that just drove me crazy. First, she began to attend a local church with the loudest pulpit pounding, screaming-Mimi Baptist preacher in the area. If that wasn't bad enough, WDCX Christian radio became her favorite station. What made matters worse was that she was listening to J. Vernon McGee and taking notes. Unfortunately for me, J.Vernon, a gravely voiced Southern preacher, was discussing what the Bible said about alcohol consumption. After that, everywhere I went in the house, Gerry Ellen posted the scriptures about alcohol.

If I went into the kitchen cupboards to get a glass I'd find posted on the inside of the door, "Do not consume wine when it moves in the glass." And on the refrigerator door were the words "Don't be a drunkard." When I would go to open the back door to head to the Val Hal La Bar, I was met with, "Like a dog returning to its vomit." One day I went into the bathroom to take care of business, and *written on the toilet paper* were the words, "Wine is a mocker of men." I wanted to find that old Texas preacher now living in California, and kick his butt!

Essentially, we came to live two different lives in two different worlds. She read God's Word and followed Bible studies on the radio, attended church, and totally changed her life to follow biblical precepts. I continued my careers as prison counselor, adjunct faculty member at two colleges, union president, crisis intervention team leader, statewide labor management committee chairman, and president of the Board of Education-all the while still serving my god: alcohol.

When you have come from the lowest gutter, a member of a motorcycle gang, a hippie immersed in drugs and alcohol, and then climbed to the top, to the very pinnacle of success… when you have grabbed the brass rail of power, prestige, and money only to find it as empty at the top as it was at the bottom, you are in trouble mister! Where do you find happiness and peace? It certainly helps to have a good job to pay the bills. However, after that it is pure vanity, smirking as it doles out a hollow reward of emptiness and despair which is even more empty and depressing than life at the bottom. At the bottom you can look up and dream of how good it would be at the top. The emptiness at the top has no remedy, only utter desolation of the soul.

CHAPTER 20

GOD'S MIGHTY HAND

—⟋⟍⟍—

Ladies, if you have been praying for your lost husbands, while suffering in a marriage that can only be described as a living hell, do not give up, do not shut up, keep praying and praying and praying some more. God will answer the prayers of a righteous wife. I realize it may be the darkest time you have ever encountered and your prayers seem to have no effect. However, know that your prayers and living a righteous Christian life will be honored by God.

Never endure physical abuse; God does not want you to be battered, or your children witnessing you being abused. Neither does He want them to be subject to abuse. The most powerful tool you have is to become a prayer warrior for your husband's soul. The fervent prayers of a righteous wife avail much. Ladies, the key is to live a life in and about Christ. Never compromise your stand on the Scriptures; bathe yourself in them, meditate on them, then go to spiritual warfare for your husband's soul. You battle not against flesh and blood but against principalities and powers of darkness in high places.

I am not telling you to post Scripture verses on the cupboards, refrigerator, doorways, or even on the toilet paper as Gerry Ellen did. However, if you abide in God's Word and the Word abides in you, you will be led to exactly what God will use to call your husband to repentance. That is my most humble prayer for you. My wife lived a life dedicated to Christ and prayed for me without ceasing for over three years. People referred to me as a pillar of the community, a living example of someone who rose from the ashes to inhabit the worldly trophy of money, power, and prestige. I was asked to speak at every type of civic and social organization, to share about how I was once a bad dude, a dreg of society who now had all those college degrees, positions, and community respect.

The only problem was that those people didn't see the pillar of the community when I would come home in a fit of drunken rage or when I would skip my children's birthdays to drink at the local bars. We are a society that values physical looks, perceptions, prestige, and wealth. Almost anyone can keep up a veneer at work, in the community, or even at church. In fact, you can keep up that veneer at church probably easier than anywhere else. However, at home you become a tyrant, an abuser, or even an abomination to those you claim to love.

As I said, keep praying, and as Winston Churchill once cried out, "Never give up, never give up, never give up."

I was asked to speak at a forum focusing on the problems within the criminal justice system. At the conclusion my fellow college professors and I went to the bar to drink and solve the problems of the world. The end result was that we got drunk, and admitted that the entire criminal justice system and society as a whole, were totally inadequate and unprepared to realistically reform and rehabilitate criminals.

When I returned home at about 3 a.m., I didn't have any idea that my life was about to be turned upside down because of the totally desperate prayers of my wife. That very night Gerry Ellen had been pleading with God to touch my hardened heart because she couldn't stand it any more. I entered the bedroom, sneaking in as quietly as possible trying not to wake her. However, when she rolled over and looked right at me, I instantly realized I needed an alibi.

I spewed out the usual lies an alcoholic uses to justify why you are drunk and coming home so late. The lies like: I got stuck talking to people who wanted my opinion on some very important issue, the car wouldn't start because I left the lights on, and, of course, the old standard, you wouldn't believe what happened! The nice thing about that one is it automatically triggers the *let me ignore this idiot, roll over, and go back to sleep* response.

I was hoping for exactly that response, however, Gerry Ellen had different ideas. This time she stared at me and with tears in her eyes and said, "I don't want to hear it no more! I-don't-want-to-hear-it-no-more!" What I didn't know was that she had been praying over and over, "God you didn't save me to live in Hell with this man, I can't stand it any more, I beg you, please touch his heart." The fervent cry of this righteous wife did avail very much!

I slipped into bed thinking Gerry Ellen would, as usual, be okay the next morning especially after venting her hostilities through that tongue-lashing about not hearing it anymore. However, I wasn't aware that she didn't just roll over and go back to sleep; she kept praying over and over for God to please touch my heart.

The next morning, which was only a few hours away, I woke up startled to find myself sitting in an upright position next to the bed staring at the clock on our bed stand which read 7:30. As I attempted to shake the cobwebs out of my consciousness, a voice filled my head sounding like a whisper yet was extremely powerful, a voice I couldn't get it out of my mind and, believe me, I tried. This small voice declared, "Get up and go to the Millgrove Bible Church, the church of your youth."

I crawled back into bed covering my head with the pillow thinking the voice must be an aberration and would certainly go away. Instead, that small voice got stronger saying, "Get up and go to the Millgrove Bible Church, I have had it with you." In stark agony I stumbled to the bathroom where I hoped a shower might wash away this nightmare and clear my mind. I remember singing, "Little voice go away and don't come back any day," to the tune of a song Gram would sing to me when we were stuck in the house during a rain storm when I was a little boy, "Rain, rain go away and don't come back until another day."

The problem was, the voice came back even stronger, "Go to the Millgrove Bible Church, this is your last chance, I have had it with you!" At that moment I realized the voice was not an aberration, it was the Spirit of God, and I had to follow His admonishment. What I didn't realize was that Gerry Ellen never stopped praying that early morning, "God you didn't save me to live in Hell with this man, I beg you, please touch his heart."

I finished showering, got dressed, and proceeded to wake everyone in the house telling them to get up and get some clothes on, because we were going to church. When our six children heard all the commotion and my call to get up they scrambled thinking, "Oh no, Dad's still drunk this morning, head for the hills!" They couldn't believe their ears, here was Dad telling them we were going to church. Gerry Ellen was astounded and couldn't believe what she was hearing. "Get up because we are going to the Millgrove Bible Church?" Wow!

I hustled all six kids and Gerry Ellen into our van and away we went. Now the devil wasn't about to just let me peacefully drive the 25 minutes it would take to get to the Millgrove Bible Church; he waged war! The kids were fighting, there were cars cutting me off, horns blaring, and people screaming at me; even flipping me the bird.

The devil knew that if anyone cut me off, giving me the standard one fingered salute, I would go into a rage chasing them until I caught them. This usually culminated with me jumping out of my vehicle, punching their side window out, and attacking them. Sometimes I would pull them out through the broken window, beat the tar out of them, and throw them into a ditch. At one point even Gerry Ellen in frustration said, "Just turn around and go home." I pulled the van over at least three times with that exact intention, to turn around and give up. However, each time that voice said "You better keep going, this is your last chance." Finally, after driving through hell we arrived at Millgrove and entered the church.

It seemed surrealistic, I was sitting in Millgrove Bible Church for the first time in what seemed like an eternity, maybe it was. Being there stretched my mind to the faded memories and wonderful times all those long long years ago. Sitting there pondering the shattered remnants of my life brought exactly what I had become into clear focus. I looked around for evidence that the building wasn't falling down on top of this sorry excuse of a man.

Legions of demons attacked with all the fury of hell torturing me with images of my hands dripping with the blood of innocent aborted babies, portraits of the fatherless children, the perversions and abominations, and the pain and suffering I had caused during vicious drunken attacks. The satanic siege was so intense I felt like bolting out of the pew and running to oblivion.

At that very instant I felt a tap on my shoulder. As I turned to see who was trying to get my attention, an aged wrinkled hand gently patted me again. There stood a lady obviously in her eighties who softly asked, "Is that you Bobby?" I was your Sunday school teacher and I have been praying for you for 35 years." She told me that my Aunt Adeline had kept her aware of what had happened to me. Oh, hot coals on my head, waves of guilt, conviction, and grief consumed me. Could I run away? The demons were screaming, "No one ever loved you, you are no good, everything you said you would never do to anyone, ha, look at yourself, you are disgusting and inflicted far worse pain!"

Within moments the service began with the singing of hymns which, of course had to be some of the very same ones I remembered from my youth. "Oh my," I lamented, "coming here was a bad idea."

That day it was announced that Pastor Dave, the Youth Pastor, would be assuming the Senior Pastor's duties the following Sunday. Pastor Dave, a graduate of Liberty University, was young, enthusiastic, and tremendously gifted with the ability to express biblical theology, precepts, and the Gospel of Jesus Christ in a manner that cut to the marrow. His sermons were like magnets speaking directly to my tortured heart.

When Pastor Dave was finishing his sermon the third week we attended church, he asked everyone to bow their heads and close their eyes. As I closed my eyes I felt a spiritual battle arise stronger than the attacks had been three-weeks earlier. Pastor Dave shared that his soul had been stirred that some attending the service felt they had done things so bad that God could never forgive them. That someone's life was full of pain, rage, alcohol, and drug abuse. The dagger of the Holy Spirit plunged deep into my soul as if that young Pastor had watched a video of my entire life. In that moment he was speaking directly to me as if I was the only person in the church.

He proclaimed that Jesus went to the cross because he loved me enough to make a full payment for those very terrible sins, before I ever committed them. Then he added, if you are that person and want to be washed in the blood of the Lamb, your sin put as far as the east is from the west and thrown in the sea of forgetfulness, come up to this altar, repent, be saved, and set free.

I vaulted from that pew running to the foot of the Cross of Calvary, crying, "Jesus, if you died for those dead babies I caused to be ripped from the womb, for the abominations I have lived, for my alcoholism, for all the terrible pain and suffering I have caused, for being a terrible husband and father, I beg you to forgive me. I repent, come into my heart Jesus, and save me."

Jesus was faithful and true, he forgave me, and a new and broken man humbly arose from that altar.

We returned home and as lunch was being prepared I went to the living room and settled into my big Lazy Boy chair with tears streaming down my face. As Gerry Ellen came into the living room and saw my tears, she asked what was wrong. I replied, "Gerry Ellen, nothing is wrong, 25 years of alcoholism is GONE, that unquenchable desire for alcohol is washed in the blood of the Lamb and I bear it no more. My god, alcohol, was crushed at the cross. Free at last, free at last, Praise GOD, Praise GOD I am free at last!" I cried an ocean of thankful tears as I basked in true freedom for the first time in my life.

I am sure you can understand why at first Gerry Ellen was a bit leery, needing to be sure I had a true heart conversion. The Bible says that with the heart one believes and with the mouth confesses unto salvation. Well, she needed to see my new heart in action. That test and verification came a week after my conversion. We were driving to the church when a carload of rather rowdy, young wise guys obviously headed to Darien Lake Theme Park, cut us off at a traffic light as they yelled obscenities out the window. I could see Gerry Ellen wince as she gauged what my reaction would be. She knew that in the past they had sealed their fate and one of my rage induced beatings was about to come upon them. However, this time, without a flicker of rage I pulled over to pray for them, my conversion was absolute. The biblical precept of bearing fruit worthy of repentance led me to see those young guys as needing mercy and prayer more than a beating. Thank you, Jesus, on their behalf, even though they never knew what you saved them from.

In the John, Chapter 2, Jesus performs his first recorded miracle when he changed the water into wine, friends, in my life he changed the wine into love for my family, and love for those young men, and love for you.

It has been 22 years since that wonderful and miraculous day. When Gerry Ellen was asked, during an interview by the 700 Club, what I was like after I got saved, she gave me a compliment and I pray may be said of me for the rest of the time God grants me to serve Him on this earth. Gerry Ellen said that the zeal I had for serving sin and darkness had been replaced by an even greater zeal to serve Jesus Christ. For whom much has been forgiven much is expected. I only desire to bring HIM fruits worthy of repentance, and nothing that didn't cost me something.

Within a few days of my coming to Christ I went to all the bars where I once raised hell and havoc and raised the name of Jesus Christ. I told everyone that I had found the answer to our pain, rage, and alcohol abuse. I humbly asked them to forgive me if I hurt them in any way. The word got out, "Alex got religion." There is nothing more threatening to darkness than the light from one whom once was so steeped in it.

I didn't mind at all telling them that Jesus in me, loved them enough to send me with the glorious truth, they can be set them free. Most of them gave me the, that's good for you routine, and scoffed as they laughingly proclaimed that they wanted to be at the party in hell with all our friends already there. I left them with a prayer and the sobering truth they already knew down deep inside: "There were no bar parties in hell, only suffering. And there were no real parties here either, only shared misery veiled by a vile laugh or two.

I finished the year out on our bowling team, drinking Pepsi and witnessing to our team. By the end of the year, after exhausting every tactic possible to test my faith, they conceded that, "This Jesus thing is real to Alex." Amen, it still is.

Back at Attica Prison the reaction was similar; everyone laughing that I had gotten religion and keeping their distance from me wherever possible. I resigned from my union leadership positions however, not before witnessing to everyone I could. I even made a special appointment to see the Commissioner of Corrections, Thomas Coughlin.

Because I received two days off work to attend to union business, which often included trips to Albany to meet with him, he was surprised when I asked for a half-hour of his personal time. He thought I was about to ask for a management position because he told me that it was alright to use prison time to see him for what he believed would be a pitch for a Deputy Superintendent job. I assured him I wasn't going to ask for anything like that, but because it was personal I wanted to use my vacation time to cover the trip. He told me just to be in his office on Monday at 9:00 a.m. and don't worry about beating him out of a few hours.

When I went into his office that early Monday morning, Commissioner Coughlin condescendingly asked, "What is so vitally important that you need a half-hour of my personal time?" Anticipating that if I didn't want a promotion I would be begging for a close friend not to be fired, I answered by saying, "What I am about to share is far more important, it is about your eternal destiny."

I sat there with one of the most powerful and prideful men in New York State sharing the Gospel of Jesus Christ. He stared at me as I told him that God was no respecter of men and even though he was extremely powerful, he had no power to save himself. I then boldly proclaimed, "Commissioner, every knee shall bow and every tongue confess that Jesus Christ is Lord, including yours and mine."

He thanked me for having the guts to come all the way to Albany, look him right in the eyes, and tell him that he needed to be saved, and that I would be praying for just that. He never repented and came to Christ that I am aware of. However, I know that God's Word never comes back void.

In 1989 there was a riot at Attica Prison when the inmates took control of all four recreation yards, burned the guard posts, and smashed windows. The rioters even tried to scale the walls in the yards in an attempt to seize control of the entire prison as happened in the infamous 1971 riot. Because I was the leader of the Hostage Negotiation Crisis Intervention Team I was immediately summoned to the prison. It was nearing 8 p.m. when I assembled my team and began the process of establishing a command and communications center. I then began the delicate and dangerous task of establishing direct contact with the rioting inmates.

Usually the Crisis Intervention Team leader directed operations from a secure command post. However, I appointed my Assistant Team leader to direct activities there. I always personally went into harm's way to assess the situation and establish primary contact with the rioters.

As I made my way through the smoke filled corridor strewn with broken glass and other debris, I realized I was in the exact spot that sparked the deadly 1971 riot. When I arrived at Times Square, I climbed up to the rooftop to begin dialog with the inmates in the yards below. That hectic process took quite a while because numerous groups of inmates were all yelling and making demands.

After letting them vent a while I convinced the inmates of two things. First, they were not going to get anyone except me to negotiate with. They demanded that the Commissioner meet with them and that news media be present. I again informed them that the only person designated to negotiate was me; no Commissioner, no media.

Second, I convinced them that each of the four yards needed to choose a committee of one black, one Hispanic, and one white spokesman to represent them, and that I would only negotiate with the committees. I told them that I would be back in 30 minutes to talk with the committees and I left to brief the Superintendent on the crisis.

When I returned to the extremely dangerous environment on top of Times Square, there were inmates climbing up onto and over those very corridors (called catwalks) where I stood. A few times I was sure the inmates would attempt to take me as a hostage. However, I was able to bluff them back by signaling to the yard tower guard as if to point out specific inmates to shoot.

What was eerie was that as I stood on the catwalks, I stood exactly where some of the hostages were held with knives to their throats during the 1971 uprising. I could clearly see the holes in the concrete where bullets had hit as State Police sharpshooters fired in an attempt to kill the inmate executioners before they could cut the guards' throats.

During my negotiations with the inmates, which lasted all night, Commissioner Coughlin and his Deputy Commissioners flew from Albany to Attica. By morning I had established enough trust with the rioters that I decided to prayerfully attempt to end the now tense drama.

The Correctional Emergency Response Team (CERT) had taken up positions on the roofs of the blocks and throughout other tactical points ready to tear gas and storm the yards. Realizing that the situation was rapidly approaching the point where the Commissioner was going to send in CERT, I did one of the craziest things a person without Jesus Christ would have ever attempted. I went out into B Yard in a last ditch effort to convince the inmates that I was putting my life on the line to stop the imminent assault of the yards.

The first thing the inmates said after being astounded that I would walk right out into the rioting yard was that they now had me as a hostage. I retorted that hostage or not, CERT was ready to storm the yards surely resulting in severe injuries or death. I stated, "We can end this now without bloodshed," and that I had my crisis team in the corridors to oversee the CERT team frisking them as they returned to their cells. As the inmate leaders met to discuss my guarantee that I personally would walk each group out of the yard and into the blocks, I heard the leaders say, "Mr. Alexander is a Christian and wouldn't lie to us, let's end this while we have a chance and before they come out here to kill us."

I walked groups of 25 inmates at a time out of the yards and into the corridors where they were frisked and escorted to their cells without one incident of abuse.

When I went to the Commissioner's Command Post after the facility was safe and secure again, Commissioner Coughlin, in front of all our facility Administrators as well as his Deputy Commissioners declared, "Alexander, you have more intestinal fortitude than anyone I have ever met. You entered yards full of rioting inmates essentially becoming a hostage and talked them into giving up!"

I replied, "Commissioner, I went out there in the name of Jesus Christ. They had to come in." He looked me straight in the eyes, shook his head, and said, "You know, Alexander; you could almost make me a Christian." I replied, "Commissioner have you ever heard of King Agrippa."

CHAPTER 21

BOTH SIDES OF THE BARS

—⁓—

It had been five years since Mark David Chapman and I parted ways. I hadn't talked to him on the few occasions I was in the Special Housing Unit. However, I was aware that he experienced some severe psychological problems not long after I was removed from counseling him, and that his wife Gloria had returned to live in Hawaii.

One sunny morning as I was on the way to the Reception Building I noticed an inmate in the recreation yard. As I walked up the stairs leading to the building, the inmate walked over to the fence asking, "Is that you Mr. Alexander?" I looked up and there was Mark.

He asked if I had recently been saved sharing that he overheard some guards talking about Alexander getting "religion." I told Mark that I was indeed gloriously saved and set free. Mark looked directly into my eyes and asked, "As a brother in Christ, did you contact that magazine all those years ago?" I told him that, "Before God, I didn't contact that magazine or anyone else, ever." Mark asked me to forgive him for wrongly accusing me. I told him that I had forgiven him five years before because knowing the truth I didn't care what he believed.

Mark shook his head in an apologetic manner as he nervously laughed sharing that he heard the new Family Reunion Coordinator was allowing Administrative Protective Custody inmates to participate in the Family Reunion Program (FRP). The FRP was the most sought out program in the entire prison system. Inmates and their immediate families were allowed a two day visit in apartment style housing units built inside the prison walls. The families were allowed to bring groceries into the visits and often barbequed on grills outside the apartments. When the family's barbequed chicken, ribs, steaks, and other tantalizing delights, it produced the greatest smells that a maximum security prison like Attica ever experienced.

Mark shared that he was extremely excited when he received the application for FRP. In his wildest dreams he couldn't imagine being allowed outside of his six-foot by eight-foot cell or tiny recreation yard constantly monitored by cameras and rifle toting guards. It boggled his mind to think of spending two days with his wife in an FRP apartment.

He shared that as he looked at the application his exuberance sank into a heart wrenching, "Oh No, Mr. Alexander is the Family Reunion Program Coordinator and he hates me!" I told Mark, that I didn't hate him and he should apply for participation in the program. After all, he had been designated cured by the prison psychiatrists, was legally married, and had been a model inmate for over nine years. When I received his application I reviewed, approved, and forwarded it to my bosses in Albany for final approval. However, with in a week it came back denied. When I asked as to the reason for denial I was told that my boss in Central Office felt we couldn't provide enough security to protect the infamous Mark David Chapman and his wife.

Wouldn't you know I was scheduled to meet Commissioner Coughlin for a lunch the very next day? As we completed our meeting agenda I asked the Commissioner why he denied Mark and Gloria access to family reunion. Because my boss, Rev. Moore knew I had influence with the Commissioner, he had tried to insulate his decision to deny Mark's application.

The Commissioner told me that Reverend Moore called asking him to sustain the denial and that he agreed with Reverend Moore; security was the only issue. I told the Commissioner that I first, would screen the other Inmates participating the same days as Mark and Gloria Chapman and could guarantee there would be no problems. Of course the Commissioner immediately challenged me asking the specifics of how I would guarantee Mark and Gloria's safety. He stated that "It would be a disaster if some one knocked off Chapman and even worse his wife." I explained that I would place my job on their safety. He instantly retorted "Why would you risk your career by guaranteeing safety of Mark David Chapman and his wife?" After all, everyone knew there were absolutely no guarantees for the safety of anyone in a maximum security prison, especially Attica.

I then explained my second strategy, which I contended virtually guaranteed safety. I was going to schedule an extremely feared and respected inmate and his wife's participation in the program at the same time as Mark and Gloria Chapman. This inmate, known as "Red" and I had gone back to the early 70's when I was a young guard in A Block and Red, a rambunctious young black militant. We experienced a few altercations in those early days, however, Red and I developed a mutual respect over the years.

The Commissioner condescendingly laughed. "Are you going to continue to guarantee the Chapman's safety and risk your job on the mutual respect with an inmate?"

I replied, "Not completely, Red is serving multiple life sentences." The Commissioner rolled his eyes as if to say, "Are you crazy, so what?" "Commissioner, I'm going tell Red, who will never see the outside of a prison wall again, that if anything happens to Mark or Gloria Chapman he would be transferred to a prison that has no family reunion program, for the rest of his life sentence." The Commissioner smiled replying, "Alexander, you're extremely good at fighting to save jobs and outmaneuvering Assistant Commissioners." The next week Mark was approved.

The day of Mark and Gloria's first visit is an experience I will never forget. I went to the Reception Building to escort an extremely nervous Mark to the Family units. As we walked from the reception building across the vast expanse inside the prison walls and over to the Family Reunion compound Mark looked like a child on his first day of school. He was stunned by the freedom of movement and spaciousness of seeing the entire inside of the prison. Having been confined to his six by eight-foot cell in the reception building for over eight years, he was a little overwhelmed by the experience.

I kept Mark in my office until the other inmates arrived by guard escort. I escorted the inmates, including Red out to their assigned units. As I left them and returned to my office to prepare to escort their families in, I pulled Red aside and before I even said a word he gave me "thumbs-up" that everything would be fine.

While checking to see if the families were at the front gate for processing I received a call on the intercom from Mark in unit #1. He asked if I could return to the unit to see him. I found him extremely anxious due to the spatial distortions of adapting to the units. We prayed, and I walked him through the entire unit and returned to my office.

With in ten minutes there was another call from Mark asking me to return to unit #1. When I arrived at the unit Mark shared that he was extremely apprehensive because it was the first time he and Gloria would be together alone since his crime. We prayed again and I assured him everything would be fine. However, I warned that if he didn't stop calling me the families would be delayed for over an hour.

I then told him to sit on the couch, read his Bible, and pray until he heard the gate by the units open.

I hurriedly raced to the prison's front gate to escort the waiting families to FRP compound just before the noon tear gas movement. I could sense Gloria's apprehension as I told her Mark was experiencing spatial difficulties however, assured her that everything would be fine and to just be patient.

Actually, everything went extremely well, Mark, Gloria, and I prayed, read scripture, and I even joined them for a lunch Gloria prepared. They have now participated in the Family Reunion Program for over 20 years.

To me, seeing families reunited was extremely rewarding, however, every now and then I had to deal with some unexpected challenges. For example, do you know what the scariest words in the world are to a male Family Reunion Coordinator? They are, "Mr. Alexander, can you come out to our unit, I think my wife's water just broke!"

When I heard those words I knew I was in trouble. Here I am inside Attica, an all male maximum security prison and a woman in Family Reunion was about to have a baby. I immediately called the prison hospital and was told that they couldn't respond to a medical problem involving an inmate's family advising me to call an outside hospital for emergency help.

Because I had five children by then I was familiar with childbirth, but only participated in one by cutting the umbilical cord with the doctor's assistance. To make things more complicated, this was the woman's first child and she was extremely scared.

I asked my Assistant and my secretary to come out to the unit to help in any way they could. My Assistant bailed out on the process so my secretary Cindy and I had to plan a strategy for delivery. We were praying that the ambulance from the hospital in Batavia would arrive before we had to attempt to deliver the child. I instantly realized we were in unchartered territory when I entered the unit to see a naked woman lying on a pull out couch made into a bed, smoking a cigarette, screaming like a banshee.

I told the husband, who was also smoking, to put both cigarettes out and get a sheet to cover up his wife. I took one look at the woman and realized we were about to deliver the first baby ever born in Attica or for that matter any men's maximum security prison. I knew we had to act fast because the baby's head was crowning. I gave mom a crash course in the breathing techniques I learned in prenatal classes when Gerry Ellen was pregnant.

Thoughts raced through my mind, "What if there were complications with mom or baby? What if the baby is unable to breathe, and how was I going to clear the mucus from the baby's mouth and throat?" I scrambled to the kitchen to find the turkey baster to use for that task to no avail as Cindy hurriedly placed a chair in front of the woman to aid in the delivery.

I exhorted the mother to give one big push and within seconds the baby popped out like she was shot out of a cannon landing right in Cindy's hands. I immediately checked the umbilical cord but didn't have to worry about the breathing passage, that baby girl came into this world screaming her head off.

Relieved that the child and mother were in good shape, I placed the baby on Mom's belly as I tied the unbiblical cord in two places using a shoe string. Just then I heard the welcome sound of the ambulance pulling up to the front of the prison. The attending paramedic's had the father cut the cord and Mom and baby were whisked away to a hospital. Whew, thank you Jesus!

After the birth of the baby, many of the guards who already referred to FRP as "The Breeding Pens," used her birth as proof that the entire program should be scrapped, because all we were doing was creating welfare babies. To me it was the only prison program that had any semblance of worth. Keeping families together was even more rehabilitating as having inmates sweeping corridors, mopping floors, or making license plates.

One afternoon I was visiting Mark in the Reception Building when he informed me that David Berkowitz had just gotten saved. He told me he asked Don Dickerman, who published Mark's testimony; to send me a copy of David's. When I received David's testimony, I placed it in my desk drawer telling Mark that I would time test his walk with Christ. I had experienced all too many false jailhouse conversions fail and wasn't quite yet ready to jump up and holler, "Praise Jesus!" However, I was more than a little intrigued considering my experiences with David while he was at Attica.

I met David when he came to Attica after pleading guilty to murder. At first he seemed stable and was actually a very likable fellow. I would spend at least three hours a week discussing a myriad of subjects from family life, to his quest to find his maternal mother, and most interesting of all, the circumstances and behaviors that led to his crimes. Using David's case and behaviors for research projects in psychology and criminal justice classes helped me graduate from RIT with honors. Like I said before I owe my Bachelor's Degree to David Berkowitz and other inmates.

During the first year of his incarceration David seemed to adapt to prison life fairly well. However, it wasn't long before he began a downward spiral. I remember an encounter I had with him just before we transferred David to Clinton Prison located in the far northern Adirondack Mountains. As I walked by his cell, I looked directly into his eyes resulting in the hair on the back of my neck to stand straight up. His cell was filthy, smelled putrid, and also hosted an array of Satanic and occult literature. He was full of darkness, looking almost like a wild animal staring right into my eyes as if I was prey. The guards told me he had been howling at night and exhibiting extremely bazaar behavior. Everyone started calling him David *Bezerkowitz* and they weren't half kidding.

I kept David's testimony in my desk for six years, and then one night there he was on the Larry King show. I intently watched the entire program, shocked by what I saw and heard. There was David Berkowitz, the Son of Sam, the crazed murderer and inmate who hissed at me the last time I saw him face to face, sitting there full of grace and peace. He answered Larry King's questions in total honesty and with the peace that only comes from God.

After watching the program, I sat down and wrote him a letter sharing my conversion and the fact that Mark had given me a copy of his testimony six years before. We exchanged letters and when I attended the yearly Magistrates Conference held near Sullivan Prison where David is now housed, I went to visit him. We had a tremendous time of fellowship in Christ and as I looked into those eyes, once so dark and tormented, I now saw peace and forgiveness. We continue to share the message that Jesus saves both sides of the bars, the guard, and the inmate.

I must share and clarify what many people have asked me about David. Do I think he should be considered for parole now that he is a Christian? My answer: absolutely not! I love Brother David however, he owes the State of New York his life for those terrible crimes where six people were murdered, and others were maimed. Give to Caesar what is Caesar's and God what is God's.

If New York State still had the death penalty and my job was that of being the executioner and David was sentenced to death, I would give him a loving hug, Christian kiss, and then carry out the execution. I would be very sad that my friend David was no longer here to share what God has done in his life, however, I know I would see him again in Heaven. I am very glad that they didn't have the death sentence in 1978 because David was saved and continues to share the good news of Jesus Christ and his mercy and grace at the cross.

Sometimes Christians don't want to believe that inmates like David Berkowitz "The Son of Sam" murderer could be saved. They often want to think that God only wants "good" people to be saved. I refer them to Saul of Tarsus, David Berkowitz, and Judge Robert Alexander. Who needs a doctor but the sick? The Bible declares that Jesus came to seek and save that which was lost. God is no respecter of people, every knee shall bow, and every tongue confess that Jesus Christ is Lord, to the glory of the Father.

As for Mark David Chapman, I believe he should be considered for parole on the same basis as every other inmate convicted of a single murder. He should be evaluated with due diligence to his crime, public safety, mental health, and institutional adjustment, nothing more or nothing less.

Mark, Gloria his wife and my family remain close friends and brothers and sisters in Christ Jesus. Even in prison, the inmate or the guard, whom the SON has set free, is free indeed. AMEN!

CHAPTER 22

HERE COMES JUDGE "A"

—ɯɯ—

Here we were a Christian family attending Sunday school, the morning and evening Church services, along with the Wednesday evening prayer meeting. Our kids were active in the youth group and all proclaimed Christ as their savior. The only person who didn't attend church with us was Grandma Du Pont. She was downright furious and viciously attacked calling us brainwashed religious fanatics. I did agree with her my brain was washed, thank God because it certainly needed a good old fashioned scrubbing. What she soon would realize was that not only my brain but my heart and soul had also been washed in the Blood of the Lamb.

The first eight months of my salvation were just wonderful. Pastor Dave was an excellent preacher and amazing teacher giving us a rock solid foundation as he explained and taught the major doctrines of the Bible. One morning he preached on Baptism as the public profession of being identified with the death, burial, and resurrection of Jesus Christ. As he closed the service in prayer he asked anyone who wanted to be baptized to raise their hands and then stay after the service. When the service ended with a hymn, I told Gerry Ellen I had raised my hand and she replied that she had done the same. We were baptized together, ahhh... it was just wonderful.

People were repenting and being saved at every service and the church was growing leaps and bounds. Now the devil couldn't stand Millgrove church being on fire for Christ, so he reared his ugly head in an attempt to tear it apart. The church bylaws called for a 70 percent favorable vote to confirm a senior pastor. A Sunday night meeting was called to vote on the Elder Board's recommendation that Pastor Dave be installed in the position.

We thought the vote would be a formality with Pastor Dave unanimously confirmed. As the Elder Board Chairman opened the meeting for comments I was stunned by what happened. In an instant, people who said they loved each other were tearing each other and Pastor Dave apart.

As if that wasn't bad enough, they also went after Pastor Dave's wife tearing her to shreds. According to these loving Christians she did everything wrong, the music she liked was bad, the way she treated people was bad, and of course the clothes she wore all came under vicious attack.

One man even attacked Pastor Dave's Mother, a person he had never met. It was ugly and the devil loved and fueled every moment of discord. The vote ended with just fewer than 70 percent of the membership voting for Pastor Dave. However, because many Church members were absent the night of the vote, the Elder Board decided to revote the following Sunday night. Gerry Ellen and I were shocked and dismayed fearing that Pastor Dave, who we loved so much, might be removed.

The following Sunday evening service was packed with almost everyone who had been regularly attending church, however, there were also quite a few people who I had never seen before. I was told that they were people who were very close to the senior pastor who had retired just before we started coming to church. They also predicted a major fight because the former senior pastor didn't like Pastor Dave, and had vowed to do whatever was necessary to block him from becoming the senior pastor.

The question and answer session was more like a combination assassination plot and filibuster, with vicious attacks on Pastor Dave and these "newcomers" who wanted to take over the church. I sat there in absolute astonishment stunned by the entire scene.

Finally I could stand it no more and rose to be heard. I asked how could the people who I heard say they loved each other every Sunday for the last eight months instantly hate each other. Was the biblical precept, you will know they are Christians by their love for each other true? And if it was, where do these vicious personal attacks and hatred fit into that agape (unconditional) Christian love.

I also asked if being the senior pastor was decided by a popularity contest or by biblical precept and if there was a biblical reason for Pastor Dave's removal. No one answered my questions, however, one Elder told me that I was too new a Christian and not mature enough in Christ to understand.

I immediately responded, "I don't have to be a Bible scholar to see hate, rage, and vicious attacks-I was a master at them before I was saved." At that point the Elders called for the final vote. Pastor Dave received less than the 70 percent needed for approval and would be removed. We were devastated; the Pastor who had led me to Christ, Baptized Gerry Ellen I along with most of our children, preached stirring messages, and taught biblical doctrines so very clearly was now fired.

I know for sure now, what I surmised back then, unity is of God, the rest; division, discord, pride, and vicious personal attacks are from hell! As I saw it there was no biblical reason to remove Pastor Dave, it was pride, and a spirit of discord fostered and fueled by Satan himself. However, if I had to do it over again I would have stayed at Millgrove Bible Church, praying for unity, rather than becoming a part of new church formed by those, including me, who became disillusioned by the firing.

We started a church named Faith Fellowship and hired Pastor Dave as senior pastor. Since that first split over 20 years ago, Millgrove has had at least one more split, and Faith Fellowship suffered a split or two as well. Because I had such a radical conversion, and experienced such a wonderful joy in my heart, I couldn't imagine walking away from God. Some people disillusioned by the split did exactly that, and stopped attending church completely. I also was too busy studying and applying the Bible to my life to have time to stay mired in despair. The devil wasn't going to be victorious in attacking me; I would stand on the rock of my salvation pressing toward the high calling of God in Jesus Christ.

At work I was promoted to Deputy Superintendent for Program Services at a new drug and alcohol rehabilitation prison. In our community I ran for and was elected as a Judge in the Village of Corfu Court. Some people have expressed amazement that after all I had done in my terrible past, I was elected as judge. So do I-but I was elected. Most people felt I would be a good judge because of my past and that no criminal would be able to con me; I had been there. Many also felt that I would be fair to all who came before me, something I have diligently strived to be.

I also completed my studies through Liberty University and became an ordained minister. There is nothing more threatening to dedicated alcoholics than one of their own former drunks and bar fighters becoming a judge, no less a Born Again Christian minister judge. However, in the Village of Corfu that is what exactly happened and it resulted in some very interesting encounters. I arraigned almost every one of my old drinking buddies from the Val Hal La Bar. These were the guys I played softball with, drank, and fought along side of for many years.

I would be called out at all hours of the night to arraign someone for driving while intoxicated, assault, or domestic disputes. Sure enough when I entered the court, there would be one of my old drinking buddies standing there in hand cuffs, drunk as a skunk with a scowl or stupid smirk on his face. Some would whine and cry that I didn't remember where I came from.

I assured them that I most certainly and vividly remembered exactly where I came from! I also reminded them that, first, I never got caught and they just did, second, I didn't drink anymore, and third, I came to the bar and shared the answer to our pain and alcohol abuse; the soul cleansing blood of Jesus Christ. Finally, I told them, "I'm going home and you are going to jail!"

What was sad was that I arraigned some of my old friends two or three times for drinking and driving. I did, however, at times utilize some innovative ways to deal with my old drinking buddies when they became belligerent. One night I was called out to arraign one of them who was extremely intoxicated and had been arrested for harassing a police officer. When the police officer escorted him into court, he began swearing at the officer and then turned his hostilities toward me.

He called me every name in his lengthy profane vocabulary. He continually interrupted the arraignment, challenging me to come down off the bench and fight him. I replied that while I would like to accommodate his request and step outside for a tussle, however, I didn't settle disagreements with my fists anymore. Now if there was ever a guy who deserved to be thrown into jail overnight, it was Rick. However, I had a much better idea. I realized a more appropriate securing arrangement would be to release him to the loving arms of his wife who detested his drinking binges. I called her at 2 a.m. explaining that I would like to release Rick to her custody, and asked if she would come to the court and pick him up.

She replied, "Certainly," as she slammed down the phone. Instantly, Rick *demanded* to be thrown in jail. NOT!

With in two minutes there was his wife dressed in her bathrobe, pink fuzzy bedroom slippers, and FIRE in her eyes. Before Rick could say a word she grabbed him by his hair, dragged him out door, and threw him in their car. As she pulled away the police officer turned to me and said, "Judge, you sure know how to dispense a little justice." I never had a problem with him again.

There was a woman in the Village who repeatedly wrote bad checks at the local grocery store. I realized she had a few mitigating circumstances including feeding her ten or so kids. The store repeatedly held the checks until she had the money to cover them. However, it got to a point where she was bouncing checks once every month or so. The store decided to press charges resulting in her and the husband being arrested because it was a joint checking account.

I didn't want to incarcerate the mother of ten children or the husband who was the sole provider for the family. I sentenced both of them to make restitution for the checks, and also perform community service by waxing the village fire trucks. The wife was less than enthusiastic as they began waxing those big bright red fire trucks, complaining, moaning, and groaning the entire time.

Finally, her husband, who had never uttered a word the whole time she was crabbing away, offered her some advice. "If you were flapping your arms, buffing as much as you were flapping your gums, we would already be home." They haven't written a bad check since.

At work I was no longer in any union position and because I was a Deputy Superintendent had to resign from the Crisis Intervention Team.

I stayed on the Board of Education for two years after my salvation then resigned. There was one thing I continued, coaching youth baseball. I chose kids for my team who were known trouble makers, many of which had little or no baseball skills. These were the kids the other coaches would never allow on their team. One baseball season a coach recruited the best players for his team then told the rest of the kids that he was sorry but they were cut from the team. I volunteered to start a team with those rejects so any boy or girl wanting to play had a team to play on.

Before the first practice I made it mandatory that a parent or guardian attend a team meeting along with their child. At that meeting I told them that I was a Christian and an ordained minister who prayed with and for the team at every practice and game. I also explained that if they didn't want their child to stay on a team coached by a Christian who actively shared his faith, I would understand. Not one of the families pulled their child from the team.

I held that team of misfits and trouble makers to the highest standards of behavior and sportsmanship. I showed them the unconditional love Jesus and I had for them. We only won one game the entire year. However, we had a great time and every kid played their heart out to the cheers and encouragement of their families who attended every game.

That year was more rewarding than the many championship teams I coached. By the way, when one of my teams won the championship, I invited the entire team and their families to attend the presentation of the Trophy at North Darien Baptist Church. I thought it would be a good way to get my team and their families to hear the Gospel of Jesus Christ. Almost the entire team and other family members attended.

To this day any time one of my former players sees me; they always stop to say hello, thank me for truly caring for them and tell me how they are doing in the most important game: the game of life. I witnessed to every player on every team I ever coached. I always prayed that when they remembered their old youth baseball coach they would remember that I was a Christian who loved them in Christ Jesus, no matter how good or bad they were in baseball or life.

I remain on the adjunct faculty at Genesee Community College which has brought about more than a few interesting confrontations. I am the only former ultra-liberal, now an ultra-conservative teaching at the college. The difference between my extremely liberal colleagues and me is that I inform my students exactly what I once was and what I once believed, compared to who I am now and why. I challenge my students to defend their positions, and even to bring anyone they desired to class to debate my positions and defend theirs. I always state my position and the roots from which it evolved. I also objectively state and describe opposite positions and schools of thought.

This is easy for me because of my background, including my extremely radical past. Most students profess the prevalent liberal ideology thrust upon them by the overwhelming number of liberal professors at the college. I easily expose how they are being programmed to align with extremely liberal philosophies and agendas by never being given a "fair and balanced," (to steal the Fox News mantra), perspective.

I am confident that when my students are objectively presented the many philosophies and schools of thought, they will make their own truly informed decisions. I also believe that when they hear the conservative positions with neutral and objective facts, they are as compelling as liberal positions. This is more than liberal students and faculty sometimes can handle. They have even brought in the Dean of the Sociology Department to evaluate my performance in class. By the time the mid-class break came she left and gave me a glowing evaluation. She applauded my openness and objectivity along with my sharing of the positions and theories with in the differing schools of sociology. I love to debunk the radical liberal philosophies that flood the college and use objectivity and facts to accomplish it.

When we study the many schools of thought and positions on religion, I invite Islamic, Roman Catholic, and Jewish clerics, along with atheists to share their theology and beliefs. I step out of my professor role and as an ordained minister represent the Born Again Christian position by sharing my testimony. I have had numerous students ask to speak to me after class resulting in the privilege of leading them to Jesus Christ. You see Nietzsche, God is alive, you are dead.

CHAPTER 23

AMEN

—⚊⚊—

Have you ever heard a Christian exhorting some one to be saved because everything in their life would just be wonderful? I shudder every time I hear that claim because "wonderful" is portrayed to mean that you will be rich, problem free, and escape despair. What biblical "wonderful" really means that God will be there whether you are abased or abound, to see you through all times, the good, the bad, and the ugly. Does not the rain fall on the just and unjust alike? I don't know about you but my life was turned upside down within a year after I repented and came to Christ. I lost my Deputy Superintendent Job due to an accident at work. The mishap caused severe damage to my back and required two operations in a ten month period.

Because I was not able to return to work within a year from the accident, I was told to apply for a disability retirement or be terminated. I chose retirement. God took away everything that I once held so dear; thought was so important and cherished. What a shock it was when my lucrative and powerful administrative position, my 32-foot cabin cruiser, luxury van, and new cars were all gone. What God accomplished was to make me totally dependant on him, break my prideful nature, and drive me to my knees.

I experienced what the song we often sing at Promise Keepers describes; "Down at your feet O Lord is the most high place." During the 16 months between the time I applied for disability retirement and received my first payment, we didn't have enough money coming in from workman's compensation to be able to pay our bills. Yet during that period, not only were we able to pay all our bills but were also able to bless a family in need with a refrigerator. God provides our needs according to his riches in Heaven.

Another example of that provision was when we were about to permanently lose my medical benefits because we needed $1,200 to pay the premium for three months of coverage in advance, God intervened. He woke Gerry Ellen up in the middle of the night directing her to look at a pamphlet about a disability income protection plan I had purchased years before.

What was amazing was that I had been told that I was ineligible for the payments by New York State. God not only directed Gerry Ellen to the pamphlet but also to the very page she was to look at. The page described exactly why I should have received the payments. She didn't even tell me she had written to the income protection plan describing their error.

Sure enough, one day before our deadline to make payment of medical insurance or lose it permanently, we received a letter from the income protection plan adminis-trator reversing the decision and declaring my eligibility. The notification included a check that provided enough money to pay the insurance for the next six months. God is so good when the times are so bad.

Beside the loss of my high-paying job and the many material possessions we had accumulated, the attack upon our family was relentless. Our kids were being drawn to the world through their secular high school peers. I certainly didn't help matters; I wanted my kids to be totally on fire for Christ, just as I was. I pushed and tugged them, trying to make them into what I wanted them to be. It took awhile to identify my pride and realize that I needed to show them a biblical father praying for them and letting them grow while seeking what God wanted them to be. I begged them to forgive me for being a Christian dictator instead of Christian dad.

Because both Gerry Ellen and I were products of totally dysfunctional families we had poor parenting skills to say the least. As a result we passed many of our own bad traits and hang-ups on to our children. Now as Christian parents we were determined to break that generational curse, heal the scars, and attempt to repair the terrible damage we inflicted on our children. Together, we studied the biblical precepts for healing and nurturing our children. The first and the hardest issue we tackled was unconditional love.

Gerry Ellen never received unconditional love from anyone until she received God's unconditional love. She had treated our daughter Jenny much like her mother had treated her. She went to Jenny begging for forgiveness and praying she could help prevent her from passing it on to her daughter Alexis. While the mold hasn't been totally broken, both Gerry Ellen and Jenny are still working to dismantle it.

As for me, I had raised my sons in barrooms. They had seen me drink, fight, and act like an idiot all too many times. I had been such an alcoholic that I had even sat my five year old son Bobby on my lap to help me steer our car home form bars.

They had seen me smash windows and walls in our house during drunken rages and skip their birthdays to go drinking at a bar. I have told them how sorry I am for being such a rotten father and have prayerfully tried to live my life in Jesus Christ in such a way that they would be proud to be my sons.

I realized a little taste of that very prayer when I ran into an old friend from the Val Hal La Bar. He had been talking to my son Brian about how I once was a bar fighter and asked him what he thought of me now that I was one of those religious fanatics. Brian told him that he likes me just the way I am now and would never want me to return to what I once was at home or in the bars.

We have come a long way in our lives in Jesus Christ, Gerry Ellen, and I, as husband and wife, parents of six adult children and now grandparents of 12 grandchildren. Our oldest son Robert II and his wife Jean are both school teachers. Our daughter Jennifer is a mother of five children. Brandon, one of our twins, is a highly decorated Staff Sergeant in the United States Marines and at this writing is in Iraq for his fifth tour of duty. Brandon's twin brother Brian, who served in the United States Air Force in Saudi Arabia, now works construction and has a son named Noah. Our youngest daughter Brandi is a court clerk, and our youngest son Joshua has decided to work in Homeland Security.

God has blessed us in so many ways. Ma DuPont came to the Lord while attending a Sunday school class I taught resulting in an amazing transformation. She told Gerry Ellen she was sorry for all the things she had done to her, but most of all, for the first time she openly told her she loved her. Ma Du Pont lived with us until she died of cancer six years after she was saved. During that time she came to think the sun rose and set on me, telling me every day how much she loved Gerry Ellen and I. When she was dying of cancer I prayed and read the Bible to her every day as she planned her burial.

She wanted to be cremated and have her ashes sprinkled on Ed DuPont senior's grave. I must admit that the way they fought and the way she had belittled him while he was alive caused me to envision a hand with a brush coming up out of his grave whisking her ashes off it.

However, I surmised that since she was saved and now such a sweetheart, even Ed wouldn't mind her there. She also wanted me to give the gospel message to her unsaved children. Just before she died she clutched my hand and told me I was like a real son to her and thanked me for taking her in when no one else would. Most of all she thanked me for loving her enough to share the Savior, Jesus with her. When she passed to glory we all were at her bed side.

Now you know we couldn't get through Ma's funeral with out a laugh or two. The first occurred when I informed the Administrator of Forrest Lawn Cemetery in Buffalo where Ed is buried, that we were going to have a ceremony and spread Ma's ashes on his grave. He informed me that it was illegal to sprinkle ashes on a grave, however, we could bury them on Ed's grave.

That was unacceptable so I decided to willfully break the law and honor Ma's request. As a judge I chuckled picturing a courtroom with the cemetery administrator telling the jury that the dust pan he held, full of wilted flowers, grass, leaves, and dirt, also contained some of the illegally scattered ashes of Evelyn Du Pont. I couldn't imagine being convicted however, if I was found guilty, would gladly accept the responsibility and punishment.

On the day of the funeral I took my chances and after reading the Bible passages Ma loved, I shared the salvation message. I then opened the plastic box and cellophane bag containing Ma's ashes and asked if anyone would like to join me in sprinkling ashes on the grave. At that point Gerry Ellen's Sister Sandy plunged her hands deep into the cellophane bag scooping up a large amount of the ashes. The only problem was that just about the time she brought her hands out of the bag along came a strong gust of wind. The ashes flew all over my brother-in-law's and my pant legs and shoes, while the rest of the family scrambled to get out of their path.

Everyone else declined sprinkling the ashes after that little glitch, so as I turned upwind and carefully poured most of the remaining ashes on the grave. After ceremoniously commending her ashes to the grave and her soul to our God in Heaven, I closed the service in prayer. As we all hugged, I had a hard time not laughing as everyone winced when they went to hug Sandy whose forearms and hands were still covered with Ma's gray ashes.

The last laugh came when Gerry Ellen wanted to stop at Wal-Mart to do a little shopping on the way home. While she went into the store, I stayed in our van with the kids, who by then were freaking out because the plastic box and cellophane bag sitting between the front seats still had some of Ma's ashes in them. In fact, some of these remaining ashes had begun spilling out onto the rug.

I decided to end the kids concern by depositing the box and bag in a dumpster located near the exit to the store. As I was walking back to our van, it hit me, what if someone finds the box and reads, "This box is certified to contain the ashes of Evelyn G. DuPont." There I was, my legs sticking out of that dumpster as I unsuccessfully tried to retrieve Ma's ashes. People came by asking if I was okay or needed help while my kids watched roaring in laughter from the van. I declined the help but gave up trying to get Ma out of the dumpster. May you rest in peace, at Forrest Lawn cemetery and the Tonawanda land fill Ma; I can hear you laugh, even now.

As for Grandma Gert, she lived with us until she was 90 years old before we had to place her in a nursing home. She had developed dementia and often arose in the middle of the night wandering up and down our road. One night she snuck out of the house at about 2:30 a.m. meandering along until she arrived at the access road to the New York State Thruway.

She walked down the access road and entered the restaurant at the Thruway service area. There she sat in her bath robe, bedroom slippers, and a fuzzy hat for hours until one of the restaurant workers asked if she wanted a cup of coffee which she gladly accepted. The worker asked why she had been there for hours with no one looking for her. She told the worker that her son Judge Robert Alexander was trying to kill her so she ran away to save her life. The State Police who brought her home enjoyed a good laugh on me as they inquired why the judge was trying to kill his mother. I replied, "I hadn't planned on it, but now I am!"

As her dementia worsened she would become frantic and claim that she heard me killing Gerry Ellen through the wall between her bedroom and our house. Sadly, we knew it was time to place her in a nursing home though we felt so guilty at the thought of her being there away from our family. However, we were forced to deal with the fact that she needed to be in the Genesee County Nursing Home when she lost all touch with reality for days at a time.

She also did some bazaar things like rubbing limburger cheese all over her face declaring that it was cold cream. One time she did the same thing with dog doo-doo. For Gerry Ellen, washing the limburger cheese off Grandma Gert's face and hands was hilarious, however, that dog doo-doo was another story. When we finally placed her in the nursing home we cried for days struggling with the reality that she was never coming home to us again.

And yet, after she was there a week or two we cried because we felt guilty for keeping her home so long. The nursing home provided great activities, programs, and excellent care. She was placed in the "Memory Unit," a name I could never understand because everyone there had little or no memory at all. Gerry Ellen and Brandi visited her every day for the entire time she was there. After a little over a year Grandma Gert decided that she had had enough of the pain in her body, stopped eating and drinking liquids announcing that she was going home to Jesus. Everyone at the nursing home loved her so much that as she was slowly dying, the nurses and other employees came to see her on their days off.

Brandi had an amazing experience with one of the nursing home residents we called "Wild Bill." Wild Bill, who was confined to a wheel chair, had an aggressive form of dementia resulting in him often physically attacking other residents and staff. He and a lady named Jamima Crab (yes Jamima Crab was her real name) often exchanged fisticuffs resulting in Bill's isolation by being placed in a day room by himself. We referred to Bill's isolation as him being in "Purgatory."

Bill had very brief moments where he was cognizant of reality, however, would experience hallucinations and dementia almost the entire day. Usually the hallucinations would have him living in a time where he was at work trying to get the employees he supervised "off their dead A_ _" and back to productivity. Everyone steered their way around Bill's wheel chair for fear of attack, well everyone except Brandi.

She wasn't afraid of Bill at all and would go right over and sit on his lap telling him she loved him and asking how work was going. Bill would chatter away telling Brandi to fire those blankety blank lazy workers. He also called Brandi by what we assumed was his daughter's name, though we never saw anyone ever visit him.

It was amazing, everyone commented on how Bill and Brandi were buddies. Normally, Bill was totally out of touch with reality and seldom if ever made a statement making any sense whatsoever. However, when Brandi was sitting in a day room with Bill while taking a break from being in Grandma Gert's room during the last three days of her life,

Bill looked right into Brandi's eyes and as clear as day said, "Your grandmother is dying!"

When mom was near death, the last words she ever uttered were to Gerry Ellen, when first, in a very weak voice, she sang, "What a day that will be when my Jesus I do see, when I look into His face the one who saved me by His grace." Then she recited John 3:16, "For God so loved the world that he gave his only begotten son, that whosoever shall believe in him shall not parish but have everlasting life."

Mom and Gerry Ellen were so close, she was the daughter mom always wanted, and mom had given Gerry Ellen love from the first day she met her. Thank you for adopting me mom and for your never failing unconditional love, see you in Heaven.

My birthmother, Marge and I have a very good relationship. She still agonizes that she had to give me up for adoption and feels guilty for all that happened to me. Recently, at a recent *Men and Women of the Harvest* conference, I honored her by washing her feet and thanked her for giving me the best gift, the gift of life. Thank you Gary Rosberg for setting the example, showing me what it means for a man to humble himself, and wash the feet of his loved ones. Such soul stirring acts can only be experienced and not described.

I have served my Savior for over 22 years, and been blessed beyond measure to be able to share the Gospel of Jesus Christ across the United States and in Canada. Gerry Ellen and I have appeared on the 700 Club and I have had the honor of sharing my testimony on many radio and television programs. We have a ministry, *Men of the Harvest* that provides food, bakery products, appliances, and vehicles to those brothers and sisters needing a hand up.

I thank God for saving me and giving my tormented soul peace. However, God decides to use this book is totally in his hands. While it is my autobiography it is actually a book about Him. All praise to the King of Kings and Lord of Lords

Jesus Christ. They say a picture is worth a thousand words, I pray these 70,000 or so words are worth a picture of God's life changing love, mercy, and grace.

And now unto him who is able to keep us from falling and present us faultless before the thrown of glory with exceeding joy, our only wise God, our Lord and our Savior Jesus Christ be all glory, honor, dominion, and power, both now and forever.

And all God's children said...

Afterward

Are You The One?

—◊◊◊—

Are you the one who I have prayed for as I wrote this book? The husband I asked God to draw to repentance and the precious Blood of the Lamb? Are you the wife who is praying for her husband and needed to be lifted up? Are you the biker, banker, inmate, guard, lawyer, or judge who is empty inside?

I would beg you to seek God's amazing grace and mercy. Maybe part of my story describes the life you are living right now and you are aching to be set free. Maybe you have never lived in darkness the way I did, but feel the Spirit of God gently tugging at your heart, calling you to Jesus. If this is you, I want you to know that I am standing with those who love you and are praying for your soul.

It makes no difference whether you are rich or poor, an inmate or a guard, a biker or a banker, a housewife or a professional woman; God does not respect one lost person above another; sin is sin, lost is lost.

You will not be judged on how good or bad, rich or poor, or even how religious you are. When you stand before Jesus Christ, the King of Kings and Lord of Lords, all that will count is whether His blood covers your sin.

My friend do you need a savior today? Fall to your knees and admit that you, like me, are a sinner and need to be saved. Tell Jesus you are sorry for your sin, then repent and turn from your path of destruction. Ask Jesus to come into your heart, and let His precious blood wash all your sin away. He will fill your heart and make you a new man or woman.

The Bible declares that after Jesus shed His blood for our sin, He died, was buried, and rose the third day. He now sits at the right hand of the Father interceding for all who come to repentance and are His.

If you have just prayed for Christ to save you, welcome to the Kingdom of God. Right now angels in Heaven are rejoicing and so am I. If I never get to meet you here on earth remember we will meet in Heaven and as it says in I Peter 2:9, "-you are a chosen generation, a royal priesthood, a holy nation, a peculiar people; that you should proclaim the praises of him who has called you out of darkness into his marvelous light."

If this book has meant something special to you, if you have given your life to the Lord, have questions, or just want to talk, we here at Men of the Harvest want to hear from you. Please visit our Internet site to learn more about Jesus or how to contact us: www.menoftheharvest.org, thank you.

In Christ Jesus,

judge a.

Printed in the United States
210457BV00001B/115-2025/P

9 781607 910947